TRANSCENDENT LOVE

Dr. Frank and Mary Alice Minirth
Dr. Brian and Dr. Deborah Newman
Dr. Robert and Susan Hemfelt

A JANET THOMA BOOK

THOMAS NELSON PUBLISHERS
NASHVILLE

For general information about other Minirth-Meier Clinic branch offices, counseling services, educational resources, and hospital programs, call toll-free 1-800-545-1819. National Headquarters: (214)669-1733 (800)229-3000

The case examples presented in this book are fictional composites based on the authors' clinical experience with thousands of clients through the years. Any resemblance between these fictional characters and actual persons is coincidental. Two of the six authors, Mary Alice Minirth and Susan Hemfelt, are not psychotherapeutic clinicians and are not associated with the Minirth-Meier Clinic. The contributions of Mary Alice Minirth and Susan Hemfelt are derived from personal experience and their contribution makes no claim of professional expertise. Portions of this book that address clinical theory and clinical perspectives do not include contributions from Mary Alice Minirth and Susan Hemfelt.

Published in Nashville, Tennessee, by Thomas Nelson, Inc., and distributed in Canada by Lawson Falle, Ltd., Cambridge, Ontario.

Scripture quotations are from the NEW KING JAMES VERSION of the Bible. Copyright © 1979, 1980, 1982, Thomas Nelson, Inc., Publishers.

Library of Congress Cataloging-in-Publication Data

Transcendent love : the fifth passage of marriage— beyond the thirty–fifty anniversary : the growth stage that can glorify your union / Brian and Deborah Newman . . . [et al.].
    p.   cm.
    "A Janet Thoma book"—T.p. verso.
    "Based on the book Passages of marriage"—CIP data sheet.
    ISBN 0-8407-4553-2 : $8.99
    1. Marriage—United States   2. Marriage—Religious aspects—Christianity. 3. Love in old age—United States. 4. Communication in marriage—United States. I. Newman, Brian. II. Passages of marriage.
HQ734.T817   1992
646.7'8—dc20   *92-33182*
                                                     CIP

Printed in the United States of America
1 2 3 4 5 6 7— 99 98 97 96 95 94 93

Contents

Acknowledgments

THE AUTHORS wish to thank the many people who helped make this book possible. Many thanks to Sandy Dengler and Catharine Walkinshaw, whose writing talents brought the illustrations, thoughts, and notes from the authors to a consistent and readable form. We also thank Janet Thoma for the many hours she spent guiding, editing, and directing the completion of the manuscript. We recognize Susan Salmon and Laurie Clark for their editorial assistance and attention to the details that helped make the book complete. Lastly, we acknowledge our children: Rachel, Renee, Carrie, and Alicia Minirth; Rachel and Benjamin Newman; Katy, Kristin, and Robert Gray Hemfelt, for the special part they add to our passages through marriage.

Chapter 1

Is Your Marriage Stuck on Base?

*C*arl Warden hated to see a grown man cry, himself least of all. But, as Beth Anne came down the aisle the tears ran freely down his cheeks. Praise God, she was beautiful! Beth Anne displayed warm, clear, suntanned skin against the white gown; long golden hair like her grandmother's, tumbling in loose waves; and that uncertain, innocent smile. She was as beautiful as his daughter Annie had been on her wedding day, almost as beautiful as Bess, his wife, had looked. Beside him, Bess gripped his arm and squeezed.

His granddaughter getting married—talk about feeling old! Carl glanced over at his daughter, Annie. The mother of the bride still had that look of I've-got-it-all-together that had made her such a source of pride to Bess and Carl all these years. She watched her daughter, dewy-eyed, as Beth Anne approached the altar.

Annie had outdone herself with this wedding. All the details, the special little touches, the attention to small things— they added up to perfection. Yes, that was Annie. Carl could feel assured Annie had done it all too. Rob, Annie's husband, provided for her well enough, but he never lifted a finger to help with anything like this. You couldn't call him lazy, but you couldn't call him a go-getter either. In all the years Annie and Rob had together, Carl could never get a really good, warm feeling for his son-in-law.

The wedding went off without a hitch; again, that was Annie and her planning. She even had the limo drivers wearing identical neckties as the wedding party moved across town to the reception at the Northside Country Club.

Bess wagged her head as she crawled into their own limo. "Can you imagine this?" Carefully she lowered herself onto the seat. "When we got married we didn't ride around in limos."

"Naw." Carl chuckled and settled in beside her. "But as I recall, our wedding vehicle cost more than this limo."

She laughed out loud. "True. A city bus does cost more than a limousine!"

The reception, like the wedding, hummed along flawlessly. Carl enjoyed being a guest of honor at a fancy "do" like this —one of the fringe benefits of old age. He shook hands with more people in two hours than he'd met in the last three years. Among them was an old business associate, Louis Ajanian. Louie, a widower, had recently remarried. He still looked in the throes of new love. Carl had never seen him quite this cheerful. Her name was Margaret.

Carl—at last—also met Julia Karris. Beth Anne had been talking about her good friend Julia for years. Beth Anne had described Julia's woes with the ex-husband, the present husband, and the kids. Too bad about all the problems. Julia was such a charming woman—graceful, dark-haired, and Julia grasped Carl's hand firmly. "Beth Anne is just gorgeous! You must be so proud."

"As an understatement, that'll do," Carl smiled.

"She's so lucky." A wisp of sadness edged her voice. "My mom never attended my weddings—either one of them—let alone my grandparents."

While the string quartet tuned up, Carl sat under a parasol and thought about this whole business of marriage. There was Louie, as happy with his bride as a pup in a dog food factory. Then there was Julia Karris, unlucky at love twice over, but still trying to make a match work. Here was Annie, who seemed to hide problems, if she had any—he bet she did. And Beth Anne, just starting out. . . . He looked across the pool at Bess. Too bad every man in the world couldn't marry a woman like Bess. It would sure solve a lot of troubles. Then the string quartet began a waltz and Beth Anne, with her groom Alan, led it off.

Everyone's marriage, a middle-aged one like Annie's, a long-lived and mature one like Carl and Bess's, and a brand new one like Beth Anne's, changes with time. So often, as in Julia Karris's case, the changes are not for the better. Some changes in marriage are predictable. The predictability of those changes enables us to recognize them and call them passages. Everyone experiences these passages at more or less the same point in their marriage. A marriage is an entity unto itself. It grows and matures in ways that are just as predictable as is a child's growth. Not all changes are governed by the inexorable march of time.

Some are forced upon you by unseen, unacknowledged secret agendas planted within every person by their past. Those unpredictable, unknown factors can improve the union. Many, though, can break the union unless they are uncovered and dealt with.

Who's Sorry Now?

Our very nature throws into marriage certain snags that we do not recognize and cannot anticipate. Those snags are generated by our families-of-origin—by the way our relatives did things, said things, and hid things. Dr. Hemfelt likens them to time-release capsules, lying dormant until something a long time in the future triggers them, and then they activate.

Several days after the honeymoon, Beth Anne and Alan stopped by Carl and Bess Warden's home to pick up some furniture for their new apartment. Alan and Carl sat at the kitchen table. Carl beamed, still a little euphoric about his granddaughter's marvelous marriage. Alan moped, like a basset hound contemplating death and taxes. He sneezed.

"Bless you," Bess called out from the kitchen sink. "Want a cold capsule?"

"Sure, anything that'll help. I'm miserable. Guess that waterskiing Beth Anne and I did on our honeymoon caught up with me. Never had so much water up my nose."

Carl chuckled. Alan studied the capsule Bess put in front of him, and the glass of orange juice. The capsule contained thousands of tiny beads, all different colors. "One of those timed release things, right?" Bess nodded.

"Orange juice is acid. Acid eats through things. What if they accidentally all go off at once?"

"I don't think it'll be a problem," Carl answered. He paused, then rose from his chair. "But just in case, we'll all be out on the patio. Let us know when you're done there."

The time-release capsules of a marriage behave similarly to Alan's cold capsule. Life may be going along routinely, your relationship comfortably chugging along. Suddenly, something triggers a time-release bead from the past. Without warning, the union is not what it was, and something has changed seemingly for no reason.

Yet these snags, and the other inevitable changes in a marriage, can be turned from bad to good once you recognize what they are.

A marriage that appears dull and mundane can be made to sparkle.

A hopeless situation can emerge into bright promise. A good union can be made better. It all depends upon finding and managing the sources of trouble, the snags and the changes. We want to help you do that.

Hints of Trouble

Couples who visit our clinic rarely come in because everything is going well. Rather, they come to see us because they sense trouble. They have needs that are not being met in their marriage. Their symptoms, the surface clues to underlying problems, show up in our case files again and again, however unique they may seem to the couples experiencing them. Because no marriage is perfect, every couple weathers these problems to some extent. But sometimes problems loom so large they threaten the union.

Look over the following hints of trouble in light of your own family relationships as you enter into the Fifth Passage of your union. Do more than a few of these hints of trouble mar your happiness right now?

Chronic Financial Distress

Why aren't Mildred and Homer prepared for retirement? They don't overspend. While not frugal, they aren't extravagant either, but their finances are wrought with debts. They're nowhere near ready to retire, and retirement is less than three years away.

There are some things, of course, that Mildred and Homer should have been doing in the years prior to this point in their lives.

They should have paid off most of their bills—ideally, all of them. They should have already scaled down their expenses for a retirement budget. Not only does that save money, it's an excellent dress rehearsal for the approaching change.

By now Homer has pretty much peaked in his career, and it's time to slow down. Yet he works even harder, putting in more hours than he did in his forties. Mildred, too, has had to take a job at the local drugstore. She'd much prefer the freedom to spend time with her grandchildren and friends, but they need the money. They're both on a feverish pace trying to accumulate as much capital as they can before Homer retires. But it's too late. They're playing catch-up on a train that keeps getting one car ahead of them with every year.

What happened? Homer knows why he can't get ahead. He's had to change jobs five times in the last twenty years because of what he perceived to be unfeeling, incompetent bosses. One of the places he worked even sent him to the company shrink to talk to him about his attitude problem. *His* attitude! Then Mildred cajoled him into marriage counseling. It took a lot of cajoling. "Counseling after thirty-five years of marriage? We're doing a lot better than the young folks who are getting divorces at the drop of a hat," Homer argued. Mildred stood firm. "Counseling or go through retirement by yourself."

After a year of counseling at the Minirth-Meier Clinic in Dallas, Texas, Homer and Mildred are still in debt, but at least now they've consolidated their debts into a workable payment plan and are on an aggressive retirement preparation plan. They're working things out. They know that retirement won't be easy, but they've accepted their financial reality and are prepared to face their future.

Homer says, "I went to a financial counselor long ago. But what I learned from him simply didn't work until my marriage smoothed out." He grimaces. "And I didn't even know it was wrinkled."

Not all financial distress points to marriage problems. We do, however, consider *chronic* financial difficulties a factor to examine closely in counseling. Another situation to consider carefully is when a person experiences constant or recurring vocational failure. This cycle often points to some individual psychological problem or anger in the marriage.

In Homer's case, he certainly wanted to be married and to support a family. It's expected of every man, and he wanted to fulfill his duty as a man. But a part of him longed for a different life, the life his father lived. His father, and even his uncle, for various reasons, had spent most of their lives supported by their wives. Homer buried that desire in his subconscious, but the echoes of his past created a time-release capsule that would appear unexpectedly. Homer was recreating his past. Homer received the message from his past, *men are supposed to be taken care of by their motherly wives.* So

Homer himself unconsciously sabotaged job after job, and blamed it on his bosses.

To us, as we work with clients, a spotty job record is a warning signal that a deeper issue may be at work. In this case Homer was saying, in a voice not even he could hear, "Yes, I've told you I want to be a breadwinner, but the echoes from my past make me feel that someone ought to take care of me."

Extended Family Problems and Involvement

A related financial clue we address is monetary dependence of the children, nieces and nephews, and/or grandchildren on a couple.

"But they're our kin! They're family and we take care of each other," a couple might protest.

Great! We're all in favor of it. Temporary financial assistance during a crisis and things like inheritances are frosting on the cake. What we look for, rather, is the prospect that the children require that money or legacy in order to survive financially. We urge couples to address situations where the retired couple is chronically financially supporting their children or other relatives.

Far more telling of a serious problem is a situation where the parents provide intense emotional support to a family member long beyond the wedding, after the married children should have loosened the economic and emotional apron strings. When parents and their children are engaged in a multigenerational family business, these particular dependencies cloud a lot of gray situations, some wholesome and some not.

Friction between the generations in general suggests that time-release capsules lie in the background of the tension. And though we will touch on time-release capsules—*unfinished business* is the more specific term—throughout this book, keep in mind for now, this broad generalization: Severe conflict and friction indicate a cross-generational problem that, if not resolved, will fester in the present generation and infect the next one.

Family Imbalance and Stress

Mabel can hardly stand to be in the same room with her husband Ralph. He grumbles and complains, she nags and nitpicks. They have no problem finding each other's faults. They do have a problem thinking of anything that the other one does right.

When family comes over, there's a temporary cease-fire. But if it's only the two of them, or even just one other person, the tension in the room is so thick you can lean on it. Mabel and Ralph fight almost every day. They wish they didn't because it upsets their kids and grandkids, just as their parents' fights used to upset them. But they have come to believe that bitter fighting is the mark of any marriage, the only way to resolve differences. Because Mabel is "right" in most of the disagreements, she makes sure the relatives are lined up on her side of the fence. Mabel uses any opportunity she can to complain about Ralph: "Your father is getting so unbearable. He's like a stubborn old ox, he'll never change. Now he won't go see a doctor. I'm afraid he's working himself into an early grave."

Their conflicts have spilled over into the bedroom. They haven't slept in the same room for years. Ralph explains, "At our age, separate bedrooms are more convenient. The fire's about out anyway. Besides, your mother snores."

In one fell swoop, Ralph and Mabel illustrate what we look for in family imbalance: chronic fighting, sexual dysfunction, factional alliances within the family ("them" against "us"), and a lack of appropriate boundaries with children and grandchildren.

Emotional or Psychological Dysfunctions

Evelyn fought chronic depression for several years. Her husband, Karl, sympathized, but he couldn't understand her attitude. After all, *he* wasn't depressed. Their marriage was fine, their economic situation stable, and their grandkids were a source of pride. Retirement for Evelyn and Karl should be fun, enjoyable, at the very least comfortable. Yet, the closer they got to retirement, the more depressed Evelyn became.

"Obviously," Karl pointed out, "it's Evelyn's problem. She's the one who needs to change. Everything else is just fine."

Only when Karl entered into counseling with Evelyn and changed some of his basic behaviors, did Evelyn start to emerge from her depression. Briefly, what happened is this: Karl, slowly, year by year, became less demonstrative of his love for Evelyn. He almost ignored her. Of course her depression didn't help the situation. Her emotional battles drove him away and turned him off. Karl's attitude and Evelyn's attitude were directly linked; married couples' attitudes always are; and their joint attitude put them on a downward spiral. As Karl became colder Evelyn became more depressed. We had to delve into Karl's past to see why he was slowly withdrawing from Evelyn. When we did this with Karl, we uncovered time-release capsules from his family-of-origin.

Karl's father typified the macho-male image—the head of family, breadwinner, but don't show any feelings, especially intimate feelings, to anyone. Karl learned this same behavior from an early age. Thus, by his father's example, he slowly withdrew from Evelyn every succeeding year of their marriage. For Evelyn, this void didn't impact her until the kids left home. Then, when it was just she and Karl, she received love from no one and that drove her to depression. There were other reasons Karl couldn't be intimate with his wife, other time-release capsules, that we won't go into in detail. For example, he had been hurt by a former girlfriend before he met Evelyn.

Once we got Karl to open up a little bit to Evelyn and show her his love, Evelyn started to recover from her depressed state.

Any emotional or psychological difficulty in one marital partner will invariably influence, and be influenced by, the other partner. Other similar symptoms we look for in marriages are: anxiety, chemical dependence and addictions, and driving compulsions such as extreme perfectionism, workaholism, spendaholism, and such.

Threats of suicide are obviously an indication of trouble.

What about You?

"There is nothing wrong with **my** marriage!" you boast. Good for you! Perhaps none of the above hints of trouble applied to you.

Would your spouse agree? Would any of these problems sound familiar to him/her? Take a moment to go over the list. Check those items that you think may apply to your relationship, even if it's just a suspicion. You don't necessarily need concrete proof. Your intuition can oftentimes be more accurate than details.

_____ Chronic Financial Distress (excessive debts, a feeling of never being able to get ahead)

_____ Extended Family Issues (overfocus on or complete disengagement from relatives and their financial and emotional problems)

_____ Family Imbalance and Stress (chronic fighting, arguments and conflict, frequent tension)

_____ Psychological or Emotional Difficulties (depression, alcoholism, perfectionism; compulsive behaviors like hoarding, eating, smoking; passive suicide—giving up on life and just waiting for death; addictions of any sort, prescription drugs for instance)

_____ Problems in the Sexual Arena (between you and your spouse or between your children and their spouses)

If you checked any of these signs of trouble, your marriage may need some help. How about your spouse? How would he or she view each trouble sign? Has your spouse ever complained or pestered you about one of these topics? Has your spouse ever seemed to go overboard with symptoms of compulsivity or depression? If so, you may have a problem you didn't know about. These issues are worth thinking about.

What Is Your Marriage Trying to Tell You?

All of the above symptoms are serious in their own right and they are indicators of underlying issues. Their presence in your marriage, and their presence in the couples we counsel, say that something far deeper than the symptom alone is going on. In this book we want to plumb the depths of problems, rather than bandage the surfaces. The dynamics, the progression through the passages of marriage, can be compared to the dynamics of a softball game.

The Dynamics of Marriage

The city league softball player steps up to the plate, shoulders his bat, and watches intently. Here comes the pitch.

"It's a solid hit into deep right field!" the announcer screams exuberantly. The ball is still airborne as the player rounds first. It drops into tall grass—*very* deep right field—and a portly fielder scurries after it. The player passes third, homeward bound.

Wait! He failed to touch second! As his team groans in unison, he runs back to stomp second base. What would have been a home run ends up only a double, all because the runner failed to clear second base satisfactorily. Marriage is like that, but we call the bases "passages."

When Doctors Newman, Newman, Minirth or Hemfelt deal with a marital problem, they deal with three entities: the husband, the wife, and the marriage itself, as if the marriage were a living, breathing organism. We have found that if a marriage, just like any living organism, is not growing, it's dying. When a marriage becomes stalled in a passage, it ceases growing. Growth is critical.

By definition, then, *passages are predictable and necessary stages, involving the physical, the emotional, and the spiritual.* Through these passages of marriage, partners journey toward the lifetime goal of growth as individuals and as a couple.

In our personal lives and in our professional practice, the six authors of this book have identified five distinct stages, passages, through which marriage passes. The developmental stages through which a child passes from birth into adulthood are well defined by theorists and are well known. Similarly, a marriage matures from developmental stage to stage—from passage to passage—roughly corresponding to the certain numbers of years it has existed. Remarriage may differ because the partners have been married previously, they might telescope a passage into a briefer time, or extend a passage beyond its normal life span.

The Passages of Marriage

Not counting courtship, which by definition is a passage of premarriage, we divide the lifetime of a marriage into five discreet units. Although some people hasten ahead of time into the next passage, or linger a little longer than average in one passage or another, in general, marriages hew to the following outline:

- The First Passage—New Love: the first two years / Whether the couple is eighteen years old or eighty, they pass first through this dewy-eyed stage of idealized love. Persons who have been married previously may go through this passage a little faster than those married for the first time, but everyone tastes its heady joy.
- The Second Passage—Realistic Love: from the second anniversary through the tenth / Kids and career put the push on the couple.
    About now, too, a heavy dose of reality sets in. This

perfect partner is not so perfect after all. If this is Eden, then why the thorns?

- The Third Passage—Steadfast Love: from the tenth anniversary through the twenty-fifth / Wrapped up in career, kids, and a host of extraneous, time-consuming activities, the couple finds themselves in a rut. Either they're mushing along complacently or they're at each other's throats, but there's a predictability about the whole relationship.

- The Fourth Passage—Renewing Love: from the twenty-fifth through the thirty-fifth anniversary / As the kids fledge and the career peaks out, the meaning and purpose of life alters forever.

     Now what?

- The Fifth Passage—Transcendent Love: beyond the thirty-fifth anniversary / What a history this couple has! The texture of the marriage changes as the couple enters retirement and youth fades for forever.

As the marriage moves from one of these passages to another—from base to base toward home plate—it also moves through specific conditions common to the human race. Crisis and conflict, intimacy, forgiveness, children, and memories form some of these conditions.

Each of the passages through which every married couple travels, like bases on a baseball diamond, must be appropriately dealt with if the next one is to count. And the tasks that accompany these passages must be completed before the next tasks commence. By tasks we mean attitude changes one must make and jobs one must complete in order to maintain an intimate marital relationship. Page 18 shows the passages and tasks that must be completed for a marriage to make it to home base.

Should a runner skip over a base, inadvertently or on purpose, dire problems result. Should a runner get stuck on one base, the only way he can leave is by walking away scoreless. Walking away is infinitely less satisfying than making it to

Major Tasks of All the Passages of Marriage

THE FIRST PASSAGE–NEW LOVE
(The First Two Years of Marriage)

Task 1: Mold into One Family
Task 2: Overcome the Tendency to Jockey for Control
Task 3: Build a Sexual Union
Task 4: Make Responsible Choices
Task 5: Deal with Your Parents' Incomplete Passages

THE SECOND PASSAGE–REALISTIC LOVE
(From the Second through the Tenth Anniversary of Marriage)

Task 1: Hang On to Love after Reality Strikes
Task 2: Childproof Your Marriage
Task 3: Recognize the Hidden Contracts in Your Marriage
Task 4: Write a New Marriage Contract

THE THIRD PASSAGE–STEADFAST LOVE
(From the Tenth Anniversary through the Twenty-fifth)

Task 1: Maintain an Individual Identity along with the Marriage Identity
Task 2: Say the Final Good-byes
Task 3: Overcome the Now-or-Never Syndrome
Task 4: Practice True Forgiveness
Task 5: Accept the Inevitable Losses
Task 6: Help Your Adolescent Become an Individual
Task 7: Maintain an Intimate Relationship

THE FOURTH PASSAGE–RENEWING LOVE
(From the Twenty-fifth Anniversary through the Thirty-fifth)

Task 1: Combat the Crisis of This Passage
Task 2: Reestablish Intimacy
Task 3: Grieve the Particular Losses of This Passage

THE FIFTH PASSAGE–TRANSCENDENT LOVE
(Beyond the Thirty-fifth Anniversary)

Task 1: Prepare for Retirement
Task 2: Continue Renewing Love
Task 3: Achieve a Transcendent Perspective
Task 4: Accept My One and Only God-given Life

home plate, for the aim of the game from the very beginning is to make it home.

Carl and Bess Warden, married forty-eight years, were making it home. As painful as eventual separation and death would be, the Wardens both would know the peace and satisfaction of being able to say, "We did it."

One of every two married couples will never know that satisfaction.

During their long life together, Carl and Bess Warden did not talk to marriage counselors or become involved in marriage therapy of any sort, though counseling might have helped them navigate the difficult passages more easily. Yet Carl and Bess did not simply muddle through. They worked diligently at their marriage, and to the very end enjoyed the fruits of a growing, timeless, abiding love.

You may be thinking, "But my marriage is so different; nobody has a husband like Joe (or a wife like Janet)."

Don't be so sure.

What If My Marriage Doesn't Fit the Pattern?

Remember the age-guessing booth at fairs and carnivals long past? A rather rough-looking man with a four-day stubble would offer to guess your age within three years. If he guessed correctly, he won and you paid him. If he missed, you won and he paid you. And he almost always won. Why? Because age makes itself known in certain ways, and the trained eye can see those ways in every person.

A marriage also ages in certain ways regardless of the people involved, regardless of the circumstances. The same patterns prevail even though yours may be a most unusual union. In fact, what is "normal"?

Mary Alice and Frank Minirth know their marriage could probably never be considered normal. "When we married, we were both in school," Mary Alice explains. "Frank, in medical school, studied day and night. I had two years yet to complete my degree, so I was studying too. It wasn't a normal start-a-family situation.

"My first job was as a teacher in inner-city Little Rock. Definitely not normal! Frank worked a twenty-five-hour day completing his internship. Then, getting a practice started— not normal. Possibly, there's no such thing as a normal marriage."

Your own situation may be less stressful than the Minirths', or more. You may be fishing off the Alaskan coast or working in a bank in Topeka. What's normal anyway? The passages themselves are the norm, the common denominators of any marriage. They form the skeleton upon which problems and pleasures attach.

Each of the authors of this book is at a different passage: Brian and Debi Newman in the Second Passage, Robert and Susan just approaching the Third Passage, and Frank and Mary Alice Minirth in the Fourth. All six of us will share with you some of our personal experiences. Drs. Newman, Newman, Hemfelt, and Minirth will share their professional expertise. In addition to counseling couples and leading marriage enrichment seminars, psychotherapists Brian and Debi put their advanced degrees to work on the staff of the Minirth-Meier Clinic. Dr. Minirth, psychiatrist and a cofounder of the clinic, takes special interest in marriage and family dynamics. Dr. Robert Hemfelt, psychologist, is well known and respected as a leader in the study of codependency and multigenerational issues.

If you've been married for many years, we want to help you examine yourself and your marriage. Did you successfully complete the passages so far? Is there something you ought to back up and re-cover? Would your happiness and contentment be fuller if you did so?

The Former Passages

Where are you and your spouse in this parade of passages? Which base are you on? To gauge your position on the ballfield, let's digress a bit and work back through the passages, back to the very beginning, when you said "I do."

The First Passage

Every couple, no matter what age they are when first married, experiences the flush and excitement of new love. This is the passage lauded by prose and poetry, linked to romanticism and idealism. Page 18 shows the tasks that a couple must master to pass first base. How well did your marriage do thirty-some years ago? Peruse the following statements to see. Check those that apply to your situation, leave the ones blank that don't. Have your spouse do the same.

1. _____ "When I think of my family, I automatically think of my husband and my children. I do not think of my parents."

2. _____ "Our relationship closely resembles a(n):

_____ autocracy

_____ democracy

_____ consensus—we come to agreement on all decisions

_____ anarchy—no organized system, chaos instead

3. _____ "I am satisfied with our sexual relationship both in the past and in the present." (Note we didn't say "resigned"; we said "satisfied.")

4. _____ "My husband/wife and I share equally in the decision making in our lives."

5. _____ "We have come to terms with any time-release capsules or unfinished business passed on to us by our parents."

How many of these statements could you check? How about your spouse? Does your relationship resemble a monarchy where one or the other of you is an all-encompassing ruler? Or is it chaos, with the two of you at each other's throats? If so, you may need to work through some First

Passage tasks and challenges. We invite you to read our first book in this series: *New Love* (Nashville: Thomas Nelson, 1993).

Conversely, if you were able to check all of the above statements and you feel your relationship is a comfortable partnership with equal participation, you probably successfully made it past first base.

The Second Passage

Rounding first base, a couple comes face to face with second base and its challenge—reality. Careers, children, and a host of extraneous activities drain a couple's time and energy. Too, each partner gets a good hard look at the person they married. This reality is too much for most marriages as the highest divorce rate hovers in this passage.

How well did your union survive this battle-torn passage? Take a moment and look over the following statements. Have your spouse do the same. Again, check the statements that apply to your unique relationship.

1. _____ "I am free to be myself with my spouse and she/he is with me. I truly know who the person is that I married and I love him/her more deeply each year."

2. _____ "We successfully childproofed our marriage. Our children do not intrude into our relationship. My husband/wife comes first, before the kids. This way the strength of the union becomes a foundation for successful parenting."

3. _____ "We have uncovered any hidden agendas, unfinished business from previous generations that plagued our relationship."

4. _____ "We have renewed our commitment to each other."

How well did your marriage complete the Second Passage? It is one of the most difficult passages to pass through. Could you check all four statements? If not, you may want to read the second book in this series, *Realistic Love* (Nashville:

Thomas Nelson, 1993) for some insights into how you can better take advantage of the bonuses of this passage.

The Third Passage

After ten or so many years together, a couple falls victim to the pitfall of this passage—complacency, taking each other for granted. To the extreme, a marriage can bottom out in dangerous codependency—a real threat in this passage. How is it avoided? By completing the tasks that accompany this passage. See how well you completed the Third Passage by checking the following statements if they apply to your particular situation.

1. _____ "My spouse and I both maintain a healthy balance between independence and dependence. I have found an individual identity within my marriage."

2. _____ "I have successfully said good-bye to my parents as demi-gods and to my mate as a knight in shining armor. I have accepted responsibility for my own God-given life."

3. _____ "I have confronted and avoided the tendency to give up and leave this relationship."

4. _____ "I practice forgiveness on a daily basis with my spouse, my friends, my parents, my kids, myself, and God."

5. _____ "I have accepted the inevitable losses of this passage: my youth, some of my dreams, and my vigor."

6. _____ "During our children's adolescence, I helped them obtain strong personal identities apart from myself and my spouse."

7. _____ "I fostered an intimate relationship with my spouse in spite of the obstacles of this passage (my self-preoccupation, for instance)."

Could you check all seven statements? How about your spouse? Great! You've reached fourth base and are looking toward home. If not, we suggest you read the third book in this series, *Steadfast Love* (Nashville: Thomas Nelson, 1993) for ideas on how you can accomplish the tasks of this Third Passage.

The Fourth Passage

Several changes during this passage act as obstacles to a relationship—the kids leaving home for good, loss of your youth and health, mid-life changes, careers winding down, and the disappointment of unrealized dreams. While this passage is not statistically marked by a high divorce rate, most couples opt for another form of separation: emotional estrangement. They divorce in spirit. Two individuals live under the same roof, with no sharing or intimacy.

How does a marriage combat these crises and emerge on a plane of enhanced intimacy? Accomplishing the tasks that follow this passage is one way. How well did you and your husband/wife do this? Look over the following statements to gauge your progress in the Fourth Passage. Before looking ahead to the joys of this Fifth Passage, you must have mastered the tasks of the Fourth. Use this self-test to help you evaluate your progress toward intimate union and renewal (the goal of the Fourth Passage).

1. "One of my very favorite romantic moments of our marriage occurred during Passage Four when _____
_____ ."
"I have talked about this moment with my spouse since then."
_____ yes   _____ no
2. "One area in which I see myself slowing physically is
_____ ."
"My spouse has noticed it."
_____ yes   _____ no
"I am embarrassed or afraid to talk about it."
_____ yes   _____ no
"I compensate for that loss by doing: _____
_____ ."

3. "When I am with friends, the topic I tend to talk about most is _____
_____ ."

"The human being whom I mention most is _____
_____ ."

"If it's not my spouse, the reason I don't mention marriage and spouse is _____
_____ ."

4. "The last time my partner and I did something truly together (not TV, unless we discussed it as we watched, interacting with each other as well as the program or video), was
_____ ."

"If it was more than a week ago, what might we have done together more recently? _____
_____ ."

5. "I [fear] [eagerly anticipate] the day our last child moves out (or did so in the past, when it happened). My major reason for feeling so is _____
_____ ."

"I have/have not discussed these feelings with my spouse because _____
_____ ."

6. "Fancying for the moment that both my spouse and I live to be a hundred with mental acuity intact, someone will undoubtedly ask, 'How did you two manage to stay together so long?' My answer would be _____
_____
_____ ."

How well did you and your spouse answer the above questions? Were there any areas that concerned you? If so, we invite you to read *Renewing Love* (Nashville: Thomas Nelson, 1993), the fourth book in this series on the passage of marriage you should have just passed through.

Once you've mastered the tasks and challenges of the Fourth Passage, your marriage is indeed on the homestretch.

You are about to score a major, major victory. If you are entering the Fifth Passage, having been together now more than thirty-five years, you are especially fortunate. The majority of marriages never make it this far.

This Book—The Fifth Passage

And now, here you are in the Fifth Passage—The final act, and then the curtain. You can stagger to the finish line, or you can run with grace and elan. Your marriage can go on hold or blossom.

Blossom? Absolutely! The six of us have learned that far from being a "downer," the Fifth Passage can be a time of joy, of release, of renewed surpassing love. Only now, with a richness of lifetime experience behind you, can you move into the indescribable comfort we call Transcendent Love.

We want to help you reach the fullness of peace and pleasure this time of life affords. We will take you along, so to speak, as we enter into counseling with clients. (For purposes of this book, we trust you understand that the characters described are fictional composites of thousands of patients treated by the doctors.) We will also draw upon the wisdom and experience of our parents and friends in this passage. By the time you finish this book, we hope to give you the tools and information necessary to truly make this the most important period of your marriage. You may find some repetition in this book from other books in this series. Since many readers will read only one book from this series, we have repeated key concepts in more than one book. If you encounter repetition, please be open to the possibility that these subjects are so vital, they bear such repetition.

One of the most important gates opening up for you right now is the gate of retirement. You will very soon, if not already, have the luxury of spending lots of time together. How best can you invest in this time together?

Chapter 2

Will Retirement Be a Boon or a Bust?

R etirement is fatal. Think about it. Every person who retires dies.

"Retirement. Bah! Twice as much husband, half as much money."

Mabel was not pleased as she sat in our office. Her husband, Emery, eight years older than she, faced retirement within two months, and Mabel was not handling it well at all.

"I don't want him underfoot all day," she complained. "No peace, no privacy. Wasting my time because he doesn't have anything to do. No. He was out with a bad back for three months a couple of years ago, and it drove me nuts."

Mabel was, for the first time, voicing a fear she had hidden from the moment she learned of Emery's pending retirement. Ever since that announcement she had suffered a series of illnesses—difficulty breathing, migraines, and stomach ailments.

Alarmed, Emery had checked her into a hospital. It was there she learned that her physical problems, which were very real, stemmed from her emotional turmoil.

Emery had some turmoil of his own. He had planned to work well into his sixties. Here he was, at fifty-three, being put out to pasture. He had started building his retirement nest egg ten years ago, thinking he'd have twenty years, at least, to invest in his future. Now he had a much smaller egg than he had planned. That hurt deeply. He was proud of the way he handled money. Now he was caught short.

Throughout their marriage, Mabel had remained essentially passive and let Emery run the show. Emery provided nicely for her. He made the financial decisions and she was glad to let him. She didn't really want to be bothered with it all. Also, Emery was set in his ways.

We asked her, "Have you ever discussed Emery's retirement with him? Have you talked about what your days should be like?"

What we were asking, in essence, was "Have you rewritten your marriage contract to accommodate this wrenching change in your life-style?"

"Why bother?" she replied. "He's a stick in the mud. He settles into something and there he stays. And he's the boss of the house; just ask him. It wouldn't do any good to talk about what I want."

Both Emery and Mabel had their work cut out for them. Emery would have to deal with his retirement. Mabel would have to become assertive enough to make her wants and feelings known. Both had important good-byes and hellos to say, and many, many adjustments to make. The first task of this Fifth Passage of marriage is, then, to prepare for retirement.

The First Task: Prepare for Retirement

Ideally, Emery and Mabel might have made some useful plans for retirement much earlier. Emery had assumed that "preparing for retirement" meant making sure you're going to have enough money.

Period. Preparation for retirement, however, entails far more than just financial plans.

Psychological Preparation

Emery started out as a coal boy on the Jersey Central railroad and worked his way up through steam locomotive engineer to diesel engineer to, eventually, dispatcher. His career spanned nearly four decades and he was justly proud of it. Now he had to say good-bye to a very big chunk of his identity. He also had to acknowledge the sad fact that his income was about to drop considerably. In a culture where worth is too often tied to income, that always comes as a blow. Emery's first big jump towards retirement, then, would be psychological.

Mabel and Emery viewed retirement as an end. Not so; it can be a beginning! It is not hard to see why it might look like the end.

Previous generations didn't have the benefits of modern medicine and financial safety nets. Their experience colors our perceptions.

Their retirement years often brought disillusionment and sadness compared with what today's retiree can expect. One random example of many: a few years ago, the man or woman (usually the woman) who broke a hip could expect to deteriorate quickly, wheelchair bound until death. Hip replacement surgery, routine today, puts that person back on a bicycle in a few months. In addition, further strides in medicine are helping us beat the osteoporosis that landed so many women in wheelchairs. Still, the gloom and doom of prior generations often gets passed on unconsciously to today's pending retirees. As the first step in their psychological preparation, Emery and Mabel had to fight that mind-set.

Of course this is not to say that life will be perfect. Consider Ralph, a retiree who dreamed of playing golf every day. He now suffers joint problems that severely restrict his swing. He must grieve the lost dream of endless hours hitting and chasing the golf ball. But he can amend his dream. Still able to walk comfortably, Ralph prowls golf courses not with a bag and clubs but with a bird book and binoculars. He added band-tailed pigeons to his life list at the Wawona Golf Course, and saw sandhill cranes flying overhead while ambling down the back nine of an Arkansas country club.

The second step: Celebrate the new opportunities in your life.

Grieve and accept the unavoidable limitations that age brings.

Amend the dream, if necessary, as circumstances require. Mary Alice Minirth is fond of saying "You have to be flexible or you'll never get anywhere."

A third major transition and adjustment in this passage is to be mentally prepared for shocks and bumps. A very damaging myth promises that two people, together for decades already, can slip quietly and friction-free into retirement. Expect some surprising rough spots; they're coming. Many psychologists claim that the life change of retirement is as great as that of puberty or of marriage itself.

Mabel and Emery were ahead on mental preparation because they absolutely knew they were facing trouble. They were unprepared for Emery's abrupt early retirement. They were especially unprepared in the financial arena. But, for Mabel and Emery, this crisis actually proved to be the saving grace for their marriage. Because of the impending financial problems, they were forced to talk about it. And talking brought them closer together.

Financial Preparation

We covered financial preparation for retirement in detail in *Renewing Love* (Nashville: Thomas Nelson, 1993), the fourth book in this series. The very latest you should begin preparing financially for retirement is in the Fourth Passage of marriage. Better yet would be preparing in the Second or Third Passages. (Don't feel bad; almost nobody else does, either.) All financial experts agree that the earlier you begin preparing for retirement, the better.

We agree too. So, by this Fifth Passage, your goal is to

maximize your finances to better enter retirement. We are not financial investment counselors, so we will not attempt to suggest strategies in that area. We highly recommend contacting a financial adviser for assistance.

But, now is not the time to begin planning. There simply aren't enough years left. You can, though, make the best out of what you have already accrued: savings, pension plan, social security, and real estate.

Whatever you do, make sure you have an accurate handle on these assets. So very often in counseling we find that one spouse is the financial wizard, and the other is totally oblivious to money matters. This is a comfortable arrangement so long as the oblivious spouse dies first. However, Murphy's Law—"whatever can go wrong will, and at the worst time"—dictates that the oblivious spouse will survive the only person who knows where all the assets are stored. Don't let that happen to you.

Together, build a theoretical retirement budget. (If you are already retired, this won't be theory.) Put down the obvious: rent, food, clothes, health and probably life insurance, basic auto expenses (insurance, maintenance), and church donations. At this point in your life you probably spend much more on the things that make life pleasant; take this into consideration in your budgeting.

Think for instance about how much you spend on restaurant meals.

Calculate a dollar amount either for the week or for the month.

_____ Breakfast at _____ for two plus tip costs $ _____.____ Multiply that total cost by how often you breakfast out.

_____ Lunch out, or box lunches at other engagements, cost about $ _____.____ Add lunches in.

_____ Dinner out can be a very special occasion. Usually, you spend about $ _____.____ total cost. Multiply that by the number of times weekly or monthly you eat dinner out.

Now add in the real zinger: other occasions. Do you get a doughnut at the mall? Soft ice cream down the street? A bag of tortilla chips to nibble on in the car? Coffee in the afternoon? A cappuccino now and then? Think about how often you usually indulge in these extras and calculate their cost.

Do you ever go to the movies? Rent videos? Attend plays and concerts? Those costs can eat into a tight budget. Consider them carefully.

If you pursue a hobby, include costs for supplies and perhaps membership in a club or group. If you don't have a hobby, we recommend you start looking for one. Hobbies are a wonderful way to keep young, to pique interest, to meet people, to enjoy life. Don't neglect to include the cost of seeking out a pleasant hobby tailored to your interests.

What in your home is going to need replacement in the next ten years? Include that cost as a lump sum or defrayed over a few years' time. (Assume the worst; that everything will need repair or replacement at some point in time.)

Spend a few hours pondering travel expenses. How much traveling do the two of you want to do? How far? By what means? Calculate ballpark figures, taking today's gasoline prices into consideration.

Is a pet or pets going to generate additional costs? Add them in. Include pet-sitting expenses if you travel.

What costs do you anticipate that are associated with:

_____ lawn care and gardening?

_____ home maintenance or condo fees?

_____ entertaining grandchildren, others?

_____ gifts for pending weddings, birthdays and the like?

_____ holidays; entertaining, decorating, cards and gifts?

_____ home entertainment; cable TV for example?

_____ church service, volunteer work, community service?

_____ health concerns and costs not covered elsewhere?
_____ postage: letters, gift parcels, mail order?
_____ telephone costs, especially long distance?
_____ taxes, levies, assessments not considered elsewhere?

Make sure you know what your monthly budget is. If your assets don't cover the budget, plan at least tentatively how you will make up for the shortfall. Should you liquidate stocks, bonds, IRAs? Perhaps one of you, or both of you, will have to work part-time. You might have to consider selling your home and moving into a smaller, more affordable one. By all means consult a responsible financial expert before doing anything major.

Don't limit yourself to just one financial strategy. Have an alternate plan waiting in the wings in case something goes wrong with your initial plan. The untimely death of one of you is a large and looming "for-instance." The wise chipmunk doesn't stash all his winter's supply of nuts in one place in the tree. He has several caches in case one of them is robbed or the supply isn't enough for a hard, long winter. In fact, these rodents make a living just out of preparing for the winter. Your situation is just as critical. To learn ways to maximize your retirement savings, seek an expert's help. If money is tight and you can't afford to pay a financial advisor, contact the local chapter of the American Association of Retired Persons (AARP) for many helpful, free pamphlets.

And again we warn you, be sure to include your spouse in this assessment. Persons who have not resolved the control issues and individuation-versus-union issues of the first three to four passages are going to slam into those unresolved problems right here, at retirement. You may have been able to put off facing certain issues for twenty or thirty years. But, when one of you reaches retirement, there will be no escaping the problem. Control and personal boundaries are the two big factors in retirement adjustments.

Control

Control issues. Boy, do they crop up now. Couples who vow they never disagreed over anything in their entire marriage will find themselves embroiled in control battles as they now prepare financially and mentally for retirement.

Mabel's best friend Doris planned to lease out her house and travel when she and her husband retired, only to learn that Bill was making a list of all the local fishing holes not intending to leave his home. Then there was Emery's pal Gus, who wanted to sell everything, live in an RV and travel all over. His wife Jeanne, had no intention of giving up her home. They had never discussed it until the day Gus suggested, "Let's go start looking at RVs," and Jeanne said "Why?" Come retirement, Jeanne and Gus literally ripped in half because they had never talked about their retirement expectations. Neither would they negotiate their dreams.

We cannot recommend strongly enough that the two of you sit down now (if you haven't already) and each discuss your dreams and expectations in the following areas:

- Where you will live (home, RV, retirement community, relative's homes)
- How much you will travel
- What activities you will be involved in (working part-time, volunteer organizations, hobbies)
- Your financial arrangements (living expenses, savings, budgets)

And, be sure that you both talk about appropriate boundaries for each other.

"Boundaries," you might say. "Isn't that what codependent people worry about?"

Boundaries, rest assured, are important for everybody.

Prepare Boundaries

Boundaries were the thing Mabel worried about most. "I don't want him underfoot all day," she said. For years Mabel had been accustomed to having her house to herself during the day, to do as she wished. She did not want to become handservant to a TV-watching-couch-potato. She didn't want to have to drop what she was doing to help Emery with some distracting project out in the garage whenever he called her. She didn't want his intrusions twenty-four hours a day.

Emery had his boundary concerns too. He didn't want the cholesterol police nagging him when he popped open a bag of potato chips and sat down to watch the sports network. He didn't want the neatness police telling him to pick up his socks and fold the newspaper when he was done with it, or to vacuum and dust and do the dishes.

Setting the boundaries for everyday life *well ahead of actual retirement* can greatly soften the impact of all the forced togetherness when retirement time comes.

We suggest you actually put some boundary agreements on paper in the form of a chart. Look over the following sections. Make them major headings on your boundary chart and then build three columns: one for you, one for your spouse, and one for the two of you together. Fill in the columns according to the wishes of both of you. If there is a conflict, work it out before filling in the chart. Simply talking about your boundary concerns can provide innovative solutions. We suggest that each of you first work through these areas independently, to determine your own needs and what you believe your spouse's response will be. Some surprising perceptual differences between you may show up. Then sit down together to compare responses and share views, and eventually to prepare the final chart. We find this an excellent exercise for improving intimacy, as well.

Space

Each person needs his or her own space to cope successfully
with the increased amount of physical and residential togetherness.

There must also be neutral space, shared as a couple. These
various spaces may be in or outside the home, but they must
exist. As an obvious addendum, we remind you that each
spouse must be willing to respect the other's territory.

His Space

Emery listed for his space: the attic for his model railroad
(Every Jersey Central retiree needs a railroad.), the tool end
of the garage, and the little office room off to the side of the
dining room. These places, of course, were certainly not off-
limits to Mabel. They were, rather, places where Emery could
pursue his own interests by himself, where he could leave
possessions as he cared to (either keeping them meticulously
neat, or slopping them about, or probably a little of both).

"My space (the husband's) should be _____

_____

_____ ."

"I think my wife would claim these areas: _____

_____

_____ ."

Her Space

Mabel claimed the spare bedroom as a workroom for her
sewing, needlework, and miniatures. There she could leave
her sewing machine set up. She could sort the skeins for her
granny square afghan without cluttering the living room. She
could put her Victorian farmhouse on sawhorses and work on
it at her convenience. Pure heaven! The kitchen, too, was
Mabel's, as was the garden-tool end of the garage.

"My space (the wife's) should be _____

_____

_____ ."

"I think my husband will claim these areas: _____

_____

_____ ."

Their Space

The living room, dining room, and bedroom constituted their shared spaces. Here Mabel and Emery could expect to interact with each other, disturb each other at will, argue or snuggle, jockey each other for the remote control, do couples things.

"Our space should be _____

_____

_____ ."

"I think my spouse would expect our space to be: _____

_____

_____ ."

Time

Time must be reapportioned as his, hers, and ours. Agree on how much time you'll be spending together and how much time will be set aside for individual use. Neither partner ought to feel chained to the other.

Both Emery and Mabel agreed they needed at least six hours each weekday to themselves. Evenings and weekends were negotiable.

Weekdays, they stayed out of each other's hair by mutual consent.

The value of the chart here, you see, was that Mabel and Emery could both visualize a workable arrangement for maintaining privacy. Seeing the promise of privacy in black and white did much to alleviate Mabel's fears and concerns.

"I think I will want _____ hours each day to myself."
"I think my spouse will want _____ hours each day."
"I believe evenings:
       _____ should be negotiable."
       _____ should be spent together."
       _____ should also have some boundaries. I'd like
      __ hours in the evening."
"I believe weekends:
       _____ should be negotiable."
       _____ should be spent together."
       _____ should also have some boundaries. I'd like
      __ hours on the weekends."

Activities

Activities should be scheduled according to two needs: the universal need to feel needed, and gratification of personal interest. Outline and share your individual activities to participate in daily, weekly, monthly, whatever. Then indicate shared activities.

His Activities and Duties

Emery decided to make breakfasts (Mabel was tired of making it after three decades and he got up earlier than she did anyway, so Emery became the breakfast chef.), keep up home repair, tinker with the car, and pursue hobbies—his railroad in particular. He also listed hunting, a seasonal activity, and the singing Christmas tree, an annual community project, as his individual activities. At last he could attend his men's prayer breakfast regularly.

"My activities and duties (husband's) will be:

_____

_____

_____. "

"My wife would like to see me do these things:

_____

_____

_____ ."

The second list need not coincide with the first. We're making plans here, not chiseling things in stone.

Her Activities and Duties

Mabel listed "cooking on whim." This was as opposed to cooking on demand. When she felt like it, she'd cook. When she didn't, they'd eat out. She also listed gardening, her hobbies, volunteer projects, the household budget (something she'd been handling for years anyway), and house maintenance not including repairs (washing curtains, steam-cleaning the carpet, sorting closets) as her duties.

"My activities and duties (wife's) will be:

_____

_____

_____ ."

"My husband would like to see me do these things:

_____

_____

_____ ."

Their Activities

As a couple, Emery and Mabel planned to attend at least one dinner (or host one) each month, go to church, take daily walks, watch certain favorite TV shows together, and make a joint library run at least once each week.

"Our activities together should be:

_____

_____

_____ ."

"My spouse would list these activities:

_____

_____

_____ ."

Goals

Given that retirement is a beginning and not an end, look closely at your goals. Husband and wife should each have several. And they should share several as a couple. When writing goals, also mention, in a few words, how those goals should be pursued. Goals definitely must provide for each other's needs. Both spouses should establish goals before entering the actual retirement phase. It is far easier to come up with acceptable goals when you're feeling good about yourself, active and working. If you are lonely, sitting about with time on your hands, goals come hard and assume less apparent importance. "Why bother?" smothers "Let's do it!"

His Goals

Emery, frankly, was quite lax about establishing goals, except for his railroad layout. He wrote short-range and long-range goals for that project, which included building a mountain, installing a whole power substation with wires, poles, and towers all over, building a master control board, and painting and arranging a herd of tiny plastic beef cattle. His non-hobby goals? "Eat." Mabel scowled at him hard enough that he added, "Finish that intensive Bible study I signed up for."

"My goals (the husband's) are:

_____

_____

_____ ."

"My wife's goals are probably:

_____

_____

_____ ."

Her Goals

Mabel determined to learn something new each day ("or you get bored with life"); volunteer for something a minimum of five hours a week; and get all the kids' stuff, stored here and there, out of her house and into the kids' houses. That would mean shipping a couple large cartons two thousand miles to Sarasota, Florida. She'd do it just to get rid of all that clutter.

"My goals (the wife's) are:

_____

_____

_____ ."

"My husband's goals are probably:

_____

_____

_____ ."

Their Goals

Provide daily support for each other (That was Mabel's idea, and Emery liked the notion of programming it right in.), keep daily activities varied to avoid boredom, and make a new best friend following the death of one of their longtime family friends.

"Our goals together are:

_____

_____

_____ ."

"My spouse would probably see our mutual goals as:

_____

_____

_____ ."

Spiritual Growth

Spiritual growth should continue until death, just as temporal wisdom grows. Not only should your spiritual dimension not be neglected, this is the time of life when it can be nurtured.

Do not neglect, either, the call for evangelism at this time in your life.

His Spiritual Needs

Emery wasn't sure he had any, other than that correspondence Bible study he'd been neglecting, and his men's prayer breakfast, both already mentioned elsewhere. And as he thought about it, that pleased him. He wasn't separating out his spiritual nature from everything else he did; the spiritual and the more mundane mingled together in his life, each enriching the other. He left that area blank.

"My spiritual needs (the husband) are:

_____

_____

_____ ."

"My spouse would probably have these spiritual needs:

_____

_____

_____ ."

Her Spiritual Needs

Mabel didn't leave this area blank. She signed up for a women's Bible study group, listed her church participation and regular duties, determined to do more for the altar guild, and pledged to bring two new people to church each month.

"My spiritual needs (the wife) are:

_____

_____

_____ ."

"My spouse would probably have these spiritual needs:

_____

_____

_____ ."

The Couple's Spiritual Needs

Emery and Mabel determined to share a prayer time daily and take the neighbors bowling once a month or so. That bowling item was an evangelistic outreach. Their new neighbors, as yet unchurched, seemed eager for fellowship and open to the word, and they loved to bowl.

"Our spiritual needs together are:

_____

_____

_____. "

"My spouse would see our mutual spiritual needs as:

_____

_____

_____ "

After you talk about these items together, build your chart. It will resemble a contract. This chart then becomes your template for everyday life. The chart offers one more chance to iron out any unresolved issues from previous passages. The chart need not be cast in cement; but its creation promotes good solid teamwork right from the beginning.

Both Emery and Mabel found that having planned activities and goals—rather than hampering freedom—actually was freeing, and surprisingly uplifting. They didn't seem to flounder about or drift. They got things done and felt good about their productivity.

Emery commented on feeling less useless, whatever "less useless" means.

A friend of ours belongs to a lifelong golf group that has grown despite its older members passing away. They meet weekly at various courses, rain, shine, or even occasional snow. They have been known to drive into a forty-mile-an-hour wind on the eleventh hole. This group serves important needs that the retired person must actively seek to fulfill. As well as offering fun, the group provides companionship.

Your activities needn't necessarily be sports. Another friend joins an informal bunch of guys on an SOS hunt. Each Thursday morning at six, they meet at a prearranged diner. They've tried nearly every diner in town. Ostensibly, they are seeking the greatest plate of SOS. "SOS", for the uninitiated, is a creamed hamburger (or other meat) mixture served over toast. The SOS is more an excuse than a reason as the men spend time in communal prayer, laugh a lot, and swap both lies and practical advice. "We talk about anything and everything," one of the group explains.

"Except cholesterol counts. Nobody is allowed to mention cholesterol." He pointed to his plate, "This stuff is a cardiologist's nightmare."

Susan Hemfelt talks of a needlepoint group that started in the 1950s as an opportunity for young mothers to visit while their babies napped. The group is still going strong, but for a different reason. Now it's a retirement support group and sometimes a crash course on how to manage with husbands in retirement.

Whether a group centers around a sport, hobby, or some other focus, a hidden agenda sustains it through the years; that is the mutual need for support in each passage of marriage.

Might some similar group serve your area of need? It's never too late to start such a group or join an existing one.

Another fount of troubles we find frequently in counseling is the situation where one spouse has had little or no outside interest throughout pre-retirement. The workaholic husband who does nothing else, or the isolated homemaker whose idea of recreation is watching TV in the afternoon, suddenly find themselves at sea, confused and aimless. Establishing goals and shoving their horizons out is absolutely essential for these people. If this is your situation sit down and think of something new to try, someplace new to explore, a hobby or volunteer project to begin. Deliberately talk about goals and purposes, and then set some. And remember, never neglect to respect your spouse's turf. His place, her place, and their place is an immensely important concept if one person feels frequently at loose ends. The temptation to infringe on the other spouse's space and time hangs heavy.

"He's always breathing down my neck," a woman named Sue complained. "I'm in the kitchen, he's in the kitchen. I work out in the yard, there he is. That's bad enough, but his criticism is the worst. He's been retired for four months now, and I've been doing my work for thirty-four years. But he thinks he knows how to do it better, or easier."

Sue was engaged in a battle just like any other military action.

Her husband was invading her territory. As an isolated homemaker, she felt suffocated by his constant presence, and yet she felt very alone due to her lack of outside interests and friends. His supposedly helpful criticism delivered the coup de grace.

Sue's husband, bored and restless, took over the chore of grocery shopping. Unfortunately, he didn't consult with Sue. Going to the store was the only time she got out of her home and he took that away from her. Sue came to us an intensely frustrated and miserable woman.

Our first effort, after evaluating their situation, was to sit Sue and her husband down to work out the orderly reapportionment of household duties. We insisted that they put duties down on paper—who would do what. This would help prevent hostile takeovers such as when Sue's husband started grocery shopping.

Second, we helped the suffocated wife develop her own interests.

Eventually, she gained enough confidence in her ability to influence her husband that she could tell him how much togetherness was comfortable for her. Achieving a comfortable balance between togetherness and separateness is a key to happiness in everyday retirement life, and it comes only with open give and take between partners.

When dissatisfaction crops up, go back to the chart to pinpoint the trouble spot. And don't expect the same chart to work forever.

As people change, so do their needs, and as needs change, so must the spouse. Revise the chart as necessary.

We hope this gives you an idea of how to build a chart for your own retirement plans. Unfortunately, such charts don't fall into place smoothly. Man or wife may balk at loggerheads over some item that simply will not respond to compromise. Then what?

Trouble in River City

We find that disagreements about major life factors respond to about the same treatment as strategies for resolving conflict.

We've covered these strategies in detail in the former passages of marriage. We assume by the Fifth Passage of marriage, you and your spouse have worked out a means for handling conflict in your relationship. If you have any doubts, or you find yourselves falling into unhealthy ways of handling conflict such as nagging, name-calling, the silent treatment, and just plain ignoring the conflict, we suggest you read pertinent sections on conflict resolution in *Steadfast Love* (Nashville: Thomas Nelson, 1993), the third book in this series. Or, pick up any book on conflict resolution at your local library. It's becoming the "thing" of the nineties, and there are lots of good titles to help you learn how to resolve conflict in your daily life.

"When you're making major life decisions like retirement and those decisions lead to conflict," says Susan Hemfelt, "a couple might resolve the conflict in one of three ways: (1) they compromise, (2) they agree to disagree, or (3) one person offers the other a love gift."

Doris and Bill, mentioned earlier, provide the example of agreeing to disagree: She wanted to take off and travel, see the kids, visit exotic places. He wanted to drown bait in all the local fishing holes, relax at home between fishing trips, and maybe plant some more roses. There was no middle ground in their case. Either you're out traveling or you're at home checking the rosebushes for aphids and tying flies. So once or twice a year, Doris goes off with friends of like interests from her bridge club. They've toured the Grand Canyon and Yellowstone, visited Montreal, and spent four amazing weeks in Australia. Bill goes fishing. Once or twice a year, he takes an extended fishing trip to some distant locale and Doris often goes along. She doesn't do any actual fishing on these jaunts. She could not care less to bob on a nauseating little boat trying to entice slimy fish to eat disgusting bait. She tours museums and parks in the area, and greets Bill at the dock upon his return.

Doris and Bill have mastered the agree-to-disagree solution. They also make certain to engage in some activity agreeable to them both, three or four times a year.

Compromise is an obvious and normal solution to conflict. By now, couples are almost always good at ironing out some sort of win-win agreement.

We find that the "love gift" solution is often misused. A love gift is when one person gives in on a point as an act of love for another. It is *not*:

_____ giving in to avoid a nasty fight or unpleasant time.

_____ giving in because you know the other person won't, so why bother trying to get what you want?

_____ giving in because it's the chronic role expected of you.

We urge every couple to monitor disagreements closely. Make certain one partner doesn't do all the love-giving and the other partner little or none. That inequality leads to resentment quickly, whether the resentment is expressed openly, or just festers inside, unexpressed, leading to depression and anger.

So far we've discussed what do to when both partners retire at about the same time. In our present culture that's becoming less common. What happens when one partner is ready to retire and the other is not?

Chapter 3

Last One in the Pool Is a Rotten Egg

U sually, when both spouses work outside the home, one retires before the other. An example is Myrtle Speis, age fifty-five.

Myrtle put in a thirty-hour work week at a water-testing lab, keeping records and billing. Eight hours each week she donated to the local library. Then her husband Murphy, seven years older, retired from his job as a mid-level air-traffic controller, and the friction started immediately.

Murphy Speis wanted to see America. He bought a motor home and customized it. He took it on a few weekend shake-down cruises. Ready to go, he insisted Myrtle retire also. Now was the time to travel, while they were both in good health.

Myrtle didn't mind travel, but she loved her job. She made good money at the lab and she liked the staff very much. It was a goofy, competent, lively, Gary-Larsonish place to work, and it made her feel young. She served as grandma to the whole lab crew, dispensing advice, bandages, and brownies as the occasion arose. She was needed. She was loved. She was loathe to give it up.

Murphy, restless and ready to go, recruited several of the couple's friends to his side of the argument. Some of Myrtle's more liberated women friends stood up for her side. The friction spread and got nastier. Before long, Myrtle could not attend a social function or even go to church without hearing that she had no right to mess up Murphy's retirement like that, or she ought to tell Murphy to go jump in a lake. A thousand times, Myrtle wanted to scream, "It's none of your business!" as people volunteered their opinions.

Myrtle and Murphy Speis, at absolute odds, could not hope to solve everything at once. Pain and resentment ran too deep by now. They untangled their Gordian knot by picking at one little loop at a time.

The allocation chart we described in detail in the former chapter worked well for this couple. The same principles apply for one-retires-and-one-doesn't situations, as it applies for mutual retirements. Before assigning them this exercise, however, we counseled them in the steps of forgiveness. Myrtle had much to forgive, and so did Murphy.

Forgiveness

Forgiveness: easy, right? You simply say to a person that you forgive them and it's done. Not so. In counseling and in everyday life, we call that quick fix "false forgiveness." These spoken words do not resolve resentment or ease conflict.

Forgiveness is such a vital part of daily life, especially in a marriage, that we emphasize this subject in all the passages of marriage. Passage One couples have much to learn about forgiveness, because they're not accustomed yet to proffering it.

By this Fifth Passage, the couple ought to be old hands at practicing genuine forgiveness on a daily basis. We find that is rarely the case. It's easy to preach; it's nearly impossible to practice.

And in this passage, as in no other, forgiveness is absolutely essential. At this stage of life, the key to happiness and peace is to come to terms with the past, the present, and the future. No person can do that without a healthy, working ability to forgive.

Forgiveness is the opposite of anger and resentment. Moreover, anger and suppressed anger (which is resentment, depression, and bitterness) are resolved only through honest, sincere forgiveness. But why forgive? Why not just forget?

Neither Murphy nor Myrtle could forget. Their minds, like yours, remember despite the best of intentions. Forgetting is therefore *not* a part of forgiveness. In fact, your body cannot forget easily. The hurts and transgressions of the past become buried deep within your subconscious mind and fester, eventually affecting your body physically. For example, long simmering anger can alter neurotransmitters in the brain.

Neurotransmitters are chemicals that help nerves transmit information between themselves. Excessive anger can alter these chemicals to produce depression, obsessive worry, and anxiety. Often you cannot simply talk yourself out of these chemically induced moods. They must be treated either psychotherapeutically from within or chemically from without, through medical and/or psychological intervention.

Forgiveness is the one sure way to resolve anger before it festers into physical manifestations. And that's not to mention the mental and emotional anguish it causes.

We have determined through our professional and personal experience that strong, effective forgiveness involves six steps:

1. Acknowledge and Admit Your Hurts.

Murphy and Myrtle had many of these, swirling around in their brains, but they had never written them down. We had them do this.

"Write down every annoyance, every little thing that bothers you relative to your marriage."

"There is not enough paper in Texas," Myrtle huffed.

"That'll be easy," Murphy replied. "But then what? If I show it to Myrtle, we'll get a divorce for sure."

"No one mentioned showing it to the other person."

This is an inventory of hurts and anger. A catalogue. Once you've done this, as did Myrtle and Murphy Speis, you can destroy the list. By getting your hurts out in the open, you see, you allow yourself the privilege of feeling them. In technical terms, you are validating your right to feel mad and hurt. You are clarifying the way you feel. Focusing. That's the first step towards resolution.

2. Commit to Forgiveness

"If we weren't committed we wouldn't be here," Murphy and Myrtle protested. It was the first thing they'd agreed on for awhile.

"We mean committed for the long term. True forgiveness is rarely a once-and-done thing."

Forgiveness does not erase the past or the effects of the past. Forgiveness must be maintained against the intrusions of that past, and that requires intense commitment.

Myrtle found that she harbored resentments she didn't even know about once she wrote out her list. Her hand couldn't keep up with the items spilling from her head. Some of them really surprised her.

For instance, there was the hurt she suffered from Murphy when she started working at the lab. Murphy never treated her job seriously. It seemed as if he didn't think she had it in her to be successful in a career after being at home all those years. He never appreciated or even realized the personal sacrifices she made for their children and family. He glibly assumed it was her duty. So when she started something different, he treated it like her hobby. No wonder he thought she should leave her job when he did his. It was her duty to him. Always her duty. And it *was* her resentment.

It took immense commitment on her part to forgive Murphy for this attitude after so many years, and to keep that forgiveness in place. The past came back to haunt her during this exercise. She certainly didn't feel forgiving. She wanted to take Murphy to task, over and over, for his callousness, for his attitude, for this past pain.

. . . Which leads us to this statement: You cannot focus

on your feelings and expect to forgive. You cannot wait to feel better about the hurt or to somehow feel in a forgiving mood, because every hour you wait, the anger festers, the bitterness forms. The pain may ease with time, but the anger does not. It simply sinks into the depths of your feelings. It will prevent the warm, fuzzy feelings you're waiting for.

3. Be Prepared to Yield

This means giving up your right for revenge or retribution. It's not an easy thing to do. When you're hurt you want to lash back. By giving this up you are turning it over to God.

We are not talking about legal contexts and obligations here. For example, the crime victim is called upon to forgive the criminal, but certainly not by withdrawing testimony or charges to stymie justice. Similarly, in divorces, a person must forgive his/her ex-spouse but not excuse that person from child support or other legal obligations.

Do you see the difference? You are to forgive the person, not the act. Myrtle forgave Murphy, but she did not have to say his actions and attitudes were right all these many years. She did not have to condone anything. That is not what forgiveness is about.

And she would have to forgive him again and again.

It takes strength and humility to relinquish this right of retribution and to expose our own hurt. Too much hate gets in the way. Frankly, true, complete forgiveness is not possible in human strength. You must accept God's help by asking for it. Call on His strength added to yours. At any given moment, with help from the Holy Spirit, a person can say, "God I want to initiate a spirit of forgiveness, now." It does not depend upon a feeling, or upon a rationale, but upon God's strength added to your determination. And it does not depend upon the person you are forgiving.

At the bottom of all this, forgiving is for the forgiver's benefit, not the forgivee's. Even if Murphy did not acknowledge that he did anything wrong, Myrtle had to forgive him. It was an act of healing for herself.

4. Be Open to the Relationship

This doesn't always apply. If you are forgiving a criminal, for example, you probably don't want a relationship with that person. (For that matter, the criminal probably doesn't want a relationship with you, either.) On the other hand, if it's your spouse, of course it applies. Myrtle now had to be open to a civil, even intimate, relationship with Murphy. It was absolutely essential if she was to overcome her anger and resentment.

Because forgiveness erases nothing, it is so often hard to warm up again to the person near and dear who wronged you. Forgiveness means choosing not to carry a grudge. The memories remain.

"I'm not sure we can be like we used to be," Myrtle mused. "Too many years, too many hurts. I don't think I can warm up to him again. And then this latest."

"You're referring to his insistence that you retire because he did."

Myrtle nodded. "Especially the part about when he started lining up his friends to get on me about it. He had old fishing buddies calling me up, telling me I was making a mistake. Can you believe it?"

We could. Murphy was desperate.

But Murphy was only half the couple. What did he have to forgive Myrtle for? Her insistence that she was going to stay with her job.

Her abandonment of him.

"But," you protest, "she didn't abandon him just because she refused to go along in that one matter."

True, we would reply. From her point of view she didn't abandon him. From Murphy's point of view, though, she was abandoning him by refusing to join his dream. Remember?

The act of forgiving is primarily for the forgiver's benefit. We called upon Murphy to forgive the wrongs *he* felt.

And so must you. It is not a matter of who is right, or who holds the most logical position. We asked Murphy and Myrtle Speis to patiently go down the list of slights and hurts they had prepared in the first exercise, and forgive each. Whether the spouse is guilty in the legal or ethical sense is beside the point. It is the hurt that must be forgiven.

Myrtle was guilty of bad attitudes and sharp words that cut Murphy deeply. In the heat of anger and argument, she said things she didn't really mean. She castigated Murphy more than he deserved for his insensitivity. She accused him of not loving her, of being incapable of real love. At one point she cast aspersions on his prowess as a lover.

For that, she had to ask forgiveness. For that, he had to proffer forgiveness.

The ones closest to you, your spouse, your children, your parents, are exactly those who are hardest to forgive. You're too close, the hurts and transgressions too immediate. You're close to them, reminded daily of what was.

But there are two others even harder to forgive than those close to you—yourself and God.

"God?" Myrtle protested. "Now you really are kidding."

"No we're not. God."

No matter how misdirected our anger may be, we get angry at God. Life is so unfair. Why did so-and-so die? Why did God allow such-and-such to happen? If He's so all-powerful, why didn't He cut a little slack for His own? In our mortal states, we lack the intelligence and foresight to understand His plans and actions. In forgiving God, we end up not forgiving Him for His shortcomings, but for ours. Remember and remember: forgiving benefits the forgiver imminently more than the forgivee.

The person hardest to forgive is yourself. Your self-talk gets in the way. You become angry with yourself, reprimanding yourself over and over. If you are like the rest of us, you are much harder on yourself than you would ever be on anyone else. Watch, therefore, for a lack of forgiveness toward yourself. Talk to yourself as you would a treasured friend, forgive yourself your mistakes and go on.

Here in the Fifth Passage, so many people realize all the wrongs they did in their lives and feel helpless to undo them.

"I feel that way," Murphy admitted. "I remember this one time, back in '67, when I just started working at the tower. The man I worked under had an alcohol problem, but he had less than a year to go before retirement. So I kept his secret with him. But he was in his cups one day—a day I was off. He made a mistake and a little prop plane almost collided with a mountain. People could have been killed. If I'd done what I was supposed to do and reported him . . ."

His voice trails off. A quarter century later, Murphy was still second-guessing a decision he made as a young man. The thousands of wise decisions he made, including some that saved life and limb, are forgotten. Murphy could not forgive himself that one sad error.

Now is the time to forgive yourself for all errors such as these and move forward. It might be well, in fact, to build a list of grievances you hold against yourself, just as Myrtle and Murphy made lists of grievances against each other. Resolve each hurt (this may involve contact with other persons, for apology or restitution), and forgive yourself.

5. Confess and Confront

This is the step where Myrtle and Murphy came face to face and talked about their hurts. *Only* do this if it feels right. There are certain areas we don't recommend discussing with your spouse.

As an example, suppose you had a fantasy, or possibly even acted out that fantasy, with another person. We don't recommend telling your spouse about this. You must work through the hurt, forgive yourself and grieve the loss of this other entanglement, but not with your spouse.

Myrtle and Murphy talked and talked about their hurts and angers. Lots of tears, hugs, and smiles later, they were well on the road to forgiving each other.

6. Put It Behind

We said that forgiving and forgetting were two different things. You've forgiven. Now if possible, forget. If that's not possible (and it probably won't be if the transgression was very serious), do whatever you can to make those memories fade. Putting it behind means:

_____ not bringing the matter up in the heat of argument.

_____ not making snide comments about the matter.

_____ not mentioning or spreading the story to others.

_____ not resurrecting it when some other hurt occurs.

God is truly the only being that forgets our sins and transgressions once we've sought out His forgiveness. He promised He would. But, you are not God.

Grieving

Hand in hand with forgiveness comes grieving as a fundamental part of daily life. In fact, you have to know how to forgive before you can grieve, because forgiveness is the last step in grieving. The Fifth Passage is as full of grieving as it is full of joy. Doing both well adds immeasurably to the quality of life older couples can enjoy.

Too, learning how to grieve is essential in a fallen world. Grieving losses is vital in your journey through the passages of marriage. Now, in this last stage, with a lifetime of losses and missed chances behind you, grieving becomes more crucial than ever.

For without grieving and resolving the losses that accompany life, you cannot embrace and hold the gains to come.

Think of your life as a glass of water. The glass can only hold so much before it overflows. If the glass is full of losses and pain, there is little room for gains and joy. By grieving, you resolve the losses and thus make room for the joys in your life. You have to get rid of the pain before you can accept any more love. As the quote goes: "A pained heart can only hold so much." We want to help you remove the pain from your heart so you can accept as much love as comes your way. This is done by grieving.

(By the way, if the glass is filled with love it never overflows. God, thankfully, made it that way. The more love we get, the more we can hold, and the more we give away. It's one of the only things that you never have too much of.)

There are five widely recognized stages of grieving that were first identified by grief pioneers such as Dr. Elisabeth Kübler-Ross. And, you have to cycle through all five before you can say that you have grieved a loss. In our vending machine world, it's far too easy to say, "I cried; I grieved that loss." We want instant gratification, instant results. But, sadness is just one stage of the grieving process. The entire process takes time which is usually directly proportionate to the magnitude of the loss you're grieving. A death, for example, may require months, even years of grieving. The loss of a treasured possession, however, may be much less.

Grieving is not the same for everyone. The magnitude of losses are felt individually. One man can be devastated over the death of his prized purebred hunting dog. Another can be just as devastated over the death of his mongrel pet. Even though the monetary value of each animal is different, the losses are just as crucial to each man. Both have major losses, each in his own way.

Dr. Hemfelt explains, "Grieving is not a one-time deal— over and done with. It is a cyclic process. Many times I caution clients that they will experience the various stages of grief over and over again. Just when you think you've resolved the loss, you might feel sadness again and find yourself cycled back into the grief process."

We had to lead Myrtle and Murphy through each step of the grieving process, for they both found they had much to grieve. Each was going to have to give up at least a few treasured desires and dreams as they approached retirement. We also helped them grieve the pain and trouble their disagreement had already caused themselves and their friends.

The five generally recognized stages of grief are:

1. Shock and Denial - Myrtle and Murphy Speis were in this stage of the grieving process when they came to us for help. This is the first stage, where you deny that anything is wrong or that you are shocked by the loss. Right after a death, for instance, most persons go through this period of shock. Myrtle and Murphy absolutely denied they had any losses to grieve.

"What losses? We don't have any. We just want to get this resolved so we can get on with our lives."

"Have either of you given up anything lately—a dream, an aspiration perhaps?"

"Well, yes. A lot of valuable time that we could have been seeing the world, thanks to Myrtle's stubbornness," Murphy said.

"And I lost all those years I could have been working, when I was taking care of you and the kids," Myrtle was quick to respond.

We told them, "Those are just some of the losses you have to grieve."

"Oh? Name another."

"How about all those hurts you catalogued? Hurts are losses."

That got them started. They even built a list of the family dogs that died.

2. Depression - Depression gets the most press of all of the stages of the grieving process. Actually it's only one step, and an early one at that. The word depress actually means "to push down." Even though we experience depression as pain, it's really an emotional numbness as the definition suggests. We shut down our feelings. Patients often describe depression

as the world becoming gray, as if the tube on the color television is broken and you're back to the old black and white image. Everything loses color and vibrancy.

Frequently during this passage of marriage, we find persons stuck in this stage of the grieving process following the death of their spouse. They might spend all their waking and sleeping hours in bed, close themselves up in the house, and spend a lot of energy just waiting, sometimes wishing, to die so they can join their loved one.

Unresolved depression can last for months or years. Brief depression is an expected and necessary part of the grieving process. Do you recall the depression that accompanied some major loss in your life?

Expect depression. A loss is a heavy load you're dealing with. It will weigh you down. Fear not, depression is almost always temporary. However, if you feel overwhelmed by the depression and it lags for a long period of time, do seek help —the counsel of your pastor, a trained therapist, and/or medical treatment.

3. Bargaining and Magical Thinking - This is the step when you'll seek some way out of the feelings of grief. We call it bargaining and magical thinking. You might try to cut a deal with God or another human being, perhaps your spouse.

"Okay, God," you say. "Get me out of this depression and I'll tithe twelve percent."

"If only I can justify the loss, I won't have to grieve it. The pain will go away."

"If only . . . ."

If you've ever thought of any "Ifs" or "If onlys," you've tried to bargain your way out of the grieving process. Again, that's normal, a natural step towards resolving the loss.

Guard though against these bargains or magical thoughts becoming courses of action. They don't work.

A woman in our counsel was doing just this after her husband's death. "If I work extra hard at the church and senior center, I won't feel as sad over Amory's death."

It worked for a while. The busyness kept her mind occupied. But it just delayed her grieving. The agony of the loss hit her again and she had to truly grieve his death. She learned the hard way, she couldn't avoid it.

4. Sadness - Sadness is what most people think of when they think of grieving, but it is only one part—this fourth part —of the process. And you can't experience true sadness if you haven't really worked through the first three steps.

Unfortunately, people try to go directly to this step of grieving. In counseling, they'll say indirectly to us, "Let me be sad for the next hour and get this out of the way." This is actually a form of bargaining: "If I cry, then I will have grieved." Again, it's the nature of our fast-paced society— instant gratification. Before you can experience true sadness (grief), however, you must have overcome your shock and denial, depression, and bargaining and magical thinking.

Luckily, memories of sorrow fade. It's one of the nicest things about the sadness step.

5. Forgiveness and Resolution - Forgiveness, acceptance, and resolution complete the grief process. Be aware that you cannot reach this step without going through the prior four steps first. Cheap forgiveness and casual acceptance resolve nothing.

This step brings a measure of peace, but it does not close the book or erase the memories. Whom would you forgive for your loss? In the case of the woman who lost her husband and was trying to bargain herself out of the grief, she had to forgive God. Why?

Remember what we said when we discussed forgiveness? She held a grudge against God for taking Amory before her and leaving her on this earth all alone. Even though that anger was misdirected, she had to forgive God for her benefit more than for His. Only then had she finally and completely grieved Amory.

Forgiveness and resolution are the light at the end of the tunnel, the cleansing aftermath of a storm, the draining of the pained feelings in your heart. Once this room has been made, more love and joy can come in.

Filling the Cup

After months of counseling, Myrtle and Murphy Speis were ready to find solutions to their problems. We led them hand in hand as they discovered the joys their new lives together could bring.

One of Murphy's biggest problems was not lack of travel but boredom. Myrtle still did the housework, as she had for years. She did nearly all the cooking. He had scant outside interests other than detailing his motor home. We suggested Murphy take over some household duties. The idea did not sit well with him. When we pointed out that this would give Myrtle more time for them to do things as a couple, he agreed to try vacuuming, dusting, KP, and half of the cooking.

Myrtle now faced a problem many such couples face. She had to assiduously avoid the temptation to take some household duties back when they weren't performed to her liking. And she had to carefully avoid criticism. They made it over that hump with a little jostling and tugging.

Because Myrtle didn't have household chores to do on weekends, she could take off with Murphy on Friday night and not return until work on Monday—sometimes Tuesday, if she made arrangements and the lab wasn't too busy. Water testing is somewhat seasonal. The weekend trips served several purposes, not the least of which was to provide them both a taste of what extensive travel would be like, with the two of them closed into a little box for hours on end.

This surprised Myrtle: The weekend trips fueled and rejuvenated their romance. Also, they needed those trips to adjust duties and roles. They even created a new plan, this one detailing exactly who would do what on the road.

We also got Murphy to extend his interests beyond the camper. A retired spouse must keep his or her day full and interesting.

Murphy could not depend on Myrtle's presence in everything; he had to carve out a retirement life of his own, independent of hers.

Besides, we pointed out, the more interests people have, the more interesting they are to others. Now was the time for Murphy and Myrtle to get a head start on the day when both would be retired.

Dr. Hemfelt warns that when one spouse retires before the other, two contracts may come into effect. Overtly, the two agree upon the details of the plan. But lurking in the shadows is another, hidden agenda neither may be aware of. The retired spouse sees what seems like a highly productive mate getting paid still, and harbors a fear of being considered useless. Resentment grows beneath the surface. The couple fight and drift apart and don't know why.

Restlessness and friction serve as signals, especially when they arise over seemingly trivial matters of finance or authority decisions. They indicate that hidden motives and fears lie below the surface. The best solution is to mutually explore one's *own* feelings. Why do I feel as I do? Talk out fears and feelings by acknowledging them. Then build a list of truths to dispel the validity of the fears.

For example, in the case above, Myrtle discovered a need to assure Murphy that he truly was needed. She was committed to him because he was Murphy, not because he had once been a mid-level manager.

She pointed out that the reason she was drawing a salary and he wasn't was that her timetable was different; she started working after he did (with time off for motherhood), and she was younger than him. Were she older, she would have retired first and he'd still be drawing a salary.

"This is true; that is not valid. I need you. I value you as a person, just the way you are." Facts and valid reassurances are the best antidote to fear and resentment.

Murphy began his retirement having no activity or interest outside that motor home. With some encouragement, he developed such a variety of interests that his dream of travel shrank down to a dream of occasional travel. Myrtle could live with that. She worked out an intermittent leave arrangement with her boss, permitting her to turn over her lab duties to a temporary worker for limited periods of several weeks. She could join Murphy then, not for travel stints extending for months and months, but for trips measured in weeks. Neither could have envisioned this compromise when Murphy first retired.

Retirement Options

Mary Alice Minirth speaks fondly of an aunt and uncle who spend their life in retirement doing things for others. "They left after Dad's funeral to go encourage an uncle in a nursing home. While my dad was undergoing cancer therapy, this same aunt and uncle bought Mom and Dad a motor home so that I could take him to the cancer center in Arlington."

And this aunt and uncle illustrate something else about finding purpose and impact in the Fifth Passage: They enjoy getting creative about it. When they see a need they brainstorm the best way to meet that need, and the idea they come up with may or may not be some tried-and-true pat answer. This is an excellent time in life to encourage new avenues of creativity.

You can no longer get paid to do what you've been doing for so many years. Suddenly, your work, your expertise, and your vast experience are no longer welcome. Your whole life, you've been throwing away possessions that were worn out and no longer useful.

Now you are the one being thrown out.

Hardly! Millions of retirees will tell that the good-bye of retirement opens a wonderful hello. Now, at last, you can do what interests you, what can help others, what can make a difference, what simply pleases you. It may or may not turn a buck, but you're bound to be rewarded.

When the Persian Gulf crisis erupted into war, Cora, trained as a "first responder," gave two days a week to the local military hospital, filling in as her training permitted for the medical personnel in the Gulf. "My war effort," she beamed proudly. Cora is fifty-eight.

Herb, a retired aviation engineer, took up whittling and woodcarving late in life. Now he teaches it at monthly sessions in an inner-city girls' and boys' club. Herb is seventy-four.

The Lacasso Boy Scout Council was going to have to give up meeting in their hundred-year-old cabin because it failed to meet building codes. John knew a thing or two about codes. He'd been a contractor for years. Enlisting the scouts themselves for labor, he and his crew tore the cabin apart, rewired, replumbed, and installed the required sprinkler system. They even rigged a burglar alarm to protect the half dozen moth-eaten stuffed mammals in a display case. They put the cabin back together and painted it to match a 1911 photo. John turns sixty-four next month.

With the major tasks of life completed—that is, nurturing the next generation and building financial security—couples in retirement are open at last to new sources of creativity and freedom. We emphasize that this is not a cookbook from which you can pick a few pat answers and plug them into your life. But we can offer some broad suggestions. Alter and shape them to your own unique needs and preferences. You and your spouse can work together in nearly all these endeavors.

How about:

Your church. The church can always use practical help with maintenance, building and repair, nursery chores, perhaps cooking, library, or gift shop work. Do youth functions need chaperons? What better chaperons/examples than a couple who have been together all these years?

Camps. Does your church, denomination, or civic group run a camp somewhere? Worthy medical charities do. Ask around. Ask especially about handicapped camps. The ratio in children's and adults' handicapped camps is often two campers per counselor or even one to one. That's a lot of staff.

Missions. Some of the most urgent needs are found in mission enterprises in our cities. You don't have to travel by camel to Timbuktu. Take the bus downtown for missions opportunities just as rewarding as foreign field service.

Hospitals. Hospital gift shops and auxiliary services use largely volunteer labor. They need responsible help. Many hospitals use people to simply sit and rock the babies in the preemie ward, for babies who are handled and cuddled grow better.

Parks. You quite possibly can spend the summer in a national park. Call a nearby federal agency to get the appropriate phone number.

Thus armed, you can call a national park and ask about the National Park Service's VIP program—Volunteers in Parks. A few parks with heavy winter visitation, such as Everglades and Death Valley, need VIPs during cold months. Most use their VIPs in the summer. The National Park Service is a division of the Department of the Interior.

National Forests increasingly appreciate volunteer help in a variety of tasks—hosting a campground, for instance. If no national forest lies nearby, call a federal agency for numbers. The U.S. Forest Service is a division of the Department of Agriculture.

You may wish to inquire also into the Bureau of Land Management and Army Corps of Engineers. They use volunteers during heavy visitation to Bureau and Corps sites such as dams and preserves.

The Nature Conservancy owns and operates a variety of

natural preserves nationwide. Look in the phone book or the library for an information number. They need caretakers and volunteers of all sorts.

Many state and city parks use volunteer help extensively. Here's a great way to think and act creatively.

Schools. Public and private schools can all use volunteers. Learning-disabled schools and halfway houses could really use your services.

Public gardens. If you prefer your fingernails with dirt under them, ask if your local public gardens need seasonal help planting spring bulbs, or weeding the begonias, or handling the annual plant sale.

The county fair, regional exhibitions, and similar expositions. For a few short weeks before and during the event, fairs need tons and tons of people to provide security in exhibition halls, man information kiosks, park cars, take tickets, pick up litter, clean restrooms, mollify lost children, answer phones, stuff envelopes, assist judges, help exhibitors set up and take down (paper work, not physical labor), assist maintenance and repair, prepare flower beds and landscape plantings, paint buildings and equipment, and help out with a hundred other little jobs. Some pay well, others use volunteer labor. Either way it's fun, and you will be making a difference.

A wealth of other opportunities. Does the zoo need docents? How about the historical museum? You know a lot of history. Can the nature center use help when school groups come through? Would the library like a grandparent type, male or female, to read to small children? Does a political candidate need someone to lick envelopes, and if so, how wet is your tongue? How about a favorite environmental or charitable organization of yours? Do they need help? Ask. Would you like to help an adult learn to read through the literacy program in your area? Do people with arthritis, people who cannot therefore hold a pen, need your help preparing taxes or filling out social security forms? Does the local animal control center or humane society employ volunteers?

What about education? Community colleges and universities are now providing senior programs aimed at your age group. It's not too late to go back to school and get trained. Or you could even take classes to learn a new craft or trade. A program catching on throughout the United States and Canada is the Elder Hostel. It provides educational opportunities for everything from working on an archeological dig to learning about Beethoven's life and works. Check with your local university or college for an information number.

A friend of ours regularly gave lectures to Elder Hostel groups in the Southwest. These groups would spend five days in a comfortable lodge on the Colorado River and learn about the natural history of the area through lectures from local experts and fascinating field trips.

What do you and your spouse enjoy doing? What are you good at? Think about it. How can you personally capitalize on those things to help others and influence the younger generation with your example and expertise? You'll never feel useless again.

Good old ex-railroad-man Emery, whom we described in detail in the last chapter, caught the idea quickly and easily. Less than a week after his retirement dinner, he lined up a class to teach steam engineers how to run their trains. His clients were the little tourist railroads in the mountains of Colorado, California, and Washington, where they assembled plenty of rolling stock, but no one knew how to operate it. He used his diesel skills on a free-lance basis, troubleshooting for a diesel generator manufacturing company. It didn't pay much, and he only got called out a couple of times a year, but it took him all over the country.

Mabel, his wife, had to grieve and accept the fact that her life was irrevocably changed. But with the grief came ample celebration.

When Emery went out on his training and troubleshooting trips, Mabel at first stayed home, rejoicing that she had the house to herself for a while. But Mabel, too, found some nice hellos. Now and then she'd go along with Emery, and she discovered she liked to travel when the trips were not too long. Most of all, she learned that by planting herself right in front of Emery and looking him eye to eye, she could tell him her wants and needs. Sometimes he even responded positively.

In essence, they rewrote their marriage contract (though neither would admit that that's what it was). They stayed out of each other's hair at specified times. They did certain things as a couple and other things independently. With a lot of juggling and shuffling, they arranged a satisfying life together. And Mabel's migraines and stomach problems disappeared.

How about You?

How well are you adjusting to retirement? Anticipating it? To see, answer the following questions. Debi Newman uses these when she counsels couples just entering retirement. Xerox this page and have your spouse answer the questions separately from you. Then discuss your results together. Are there any areas you need to emphasize on your retirement plan? If you haven't prepared a chart much like we discussed in the last chapter, you may find you don't agree with each other on these answers. That's why we highly recommend you prepare a retirement plan and allocation chart together.

1. (True or False) I enjoy the job I have and do not believe that it conflicts with our marital happiness.
2. (True or False) I am having a hard time adjusting to retirement or planning for retirement because my job has been such a central aspect of my life.
3. (True or False) I frequently feel jealous of my spouse's job.
4. (True or False) I am satisfied with the way we balance work and marriage.
5. (True or False) I am afraid of the new stresses retirement will bring to our marriage.

6. (True or False) I am the type of person who will need lots of things to keep me busy after retirement.
7. (True or False) I just want to sit and relax after retirement.
8. (True or False) I'm afraid that I will appear lazy compared to my partner after we both retire. I enjoy relaxing while he/she is very active.
9. (True or False) I am willing to allow my partner the time and encouragement to do what is important to him/her after retirement.

Just as much as retirement changes your life, so can the next generations. Grandchildren and adult children's influences on your marriage can either enhance or detract from your relationship. How your relationship is impacted depends on you.

Chapter 4

The Period of Joy

C ody is one of those kids grandparents euphemistically label "all boy." Tough? When he walks in the forest, wolves hide. Crude? When he belches, dishes rattle. Active? His constant buzz of frenetic motion alters weather patterns. And the kid's only five. Just wait until he's twelve.

They quit taking him to restaurants when he threw peas at the man across the way. He was scoring eighty percent hits, but his parents weren't impressed. Neither was the man. Ever since he caused the runaway at the pony rides they've been afraid to take him to the amusement park. And after that fire department call to the neighbor's house, the station captain tactfully requested that the hostess of Cody's friend's birthday party spread the word: whatever you do, don't invite Cody.

Cody sees his grandparents at least once a week and sometimes more often, depending on how long his parents can live with him before they need a rest. Cody's grandparents are not just baby-sitting. They are being dumped upon.

Cody underscores a potential trouble spot we find frequently emerging in this Fifth Passage of marriage, the interference in the couple's daily life posed by adult children and grandchildren.

"But," you might protest, "my grandchildren are truly a joy."

And that is definitely true. Grandchildren are one of the nicest things that happen to us during this stage of our lives.

The Shifting Sands of Parenthood

As rapidly as a newborn child changes, the parents change also. And the maturation is quite as predictable and certain in the parent as in the child. This maturation can be broken down into five stages, which do not parallel the actual passages of marriage.

The first four stages (period of surprise—the first child; period of drifting—school-age children; period of turmoil—the teenager; and, death of a relationship—the empty nest) were covered in our former books on the Second, Third, and Fourth Passages of marriage. The last stage, the period of joy (grandchildren), is covered here.

Joy. Unless your grandchild is Cody.

The Children's Children

This final stage in the progression of parenthood is enjoyable in many different ways. Certainly, the numerous people who have to look at "pictures of my grandchildren" see a pride that may, at times, seem overly enthusiastic.

"Children's children are the crown of old men," says Proverbs 17:6. Ask the mother of the first grandchild in the family, any family. Often these tiny bundles resemble the grandparent's own child, so the experience is the closest any of us will ever get to drinking from that proverbial fountain of youth. Any interaction with these miniatures of your son or daughter is like turning the clock back and recapturing those moments together.

Excitement and joy and love abound! God designed it that way. And perhaps the greatest joy is that you can spoil them and then send them back to their parents. "If I had known grandchildren were so much fun, I would have had them first," says the old barb. But if solid, comfortable boundaries are not in place, grandchildren and adult children can become too much of a good thing.

Setting Boundaries

Once or twice a week, May and Gary get a call from their daughter.

"I'm bringing Cody over, okay? I have to go to the dentist, and I can't leave him alone in the waiting room."

It's certainly a sound reason, considering what happened to the tropical fish in a doctor's waiting room last winter. Cody can't be trusted even with an anchor chained to his wrist. May's daughter always has a good, solid, practical reason why she can't take Cody with her. Never frivolous reasons. And when your daughter really, truly needs something, you certainly cannot say no. It's usually on short notice; the daughter explains her regular baby-sitting arrangement fell through, or the appointment was moved up, or the car is in the garage, or . . . .

And so May and Gary put their own plans on hold and take Cody. You do not go places with Cody. You do not pursue hobbies with Cody because hobbies divert your attention. Cody needs but moments of inattention to destroy something.

May and Gary suffer—and with Cody, "suffer" is a word used not inappropriately—a problem we see very, very frequently in the lives of older persons. The retired couple find themselves curtailing their own plans as they serve as hosts, baby-sitters, or emergency counselors. To an extent, this is good; older people have a wisdom and balance that youth need.

How much is too much and what do you do about it? Every situation is unique, including yours. You must work out the boundaries yourself.

Dr. Deborah Newman explains, "A couple must agree on boundaries with their adult children. Sit down together. Even put it on paper. It's absolutely imperative. Otherwise, the couple gets embroiled in conflict, either with each other or with the kids." Either way, the marriage suffers.

"To start a couple on setting boundaries, we ask them to think about the big things first. Items like baby-sitting, financial support, and visiting. Once they've thought these areas through individually, we ask them to discuss it together. Then we lead them through an exercise in preparing boundaries."

You, too, can use this process. First, each grandparent answers the following questions separately. Then the grandparents come together to discuss the results. The adult children do the same.

Then grandparents and adult children come together, discuss the answers, and set up a working contract based on needs, desires, and compromises.

We recommend that you do this even if you don't have grandchildren yet. Forewarned is much better than being caught off guard.

1. How do you feel about grandparents baby-sitting for the grandchildren?
2. How do you feel about grandparents giving gifts of money to the adult children or grandchildren?
3. How do you feel about the grandparents financially supporting the adult children or grandchildren?
4. How often should grandparents call or visit their grandchildren?
5. How often should grandchildren call or visit the grandparents?

Once you've discussed these questions in depth together, you can fill in the following sentences to help you define the parameters of your relationship with your children and grandchildren.

"We will baby-sit the grandchildren _____ times per (week)

(month)." (Inherent in this statement is another statement, "The adult children will plan so as to use the agreed-upon times and not pop in with 'emergencies.' ")

"We will entertain any requests for money from our children or grandchildren. That does not mean we will always be able to grant them. Amounts over ____ will require partial or full repayment, based on a mutually acceptable payment plan."

"We will try to be equitable in financial gifts to our children and grandchildren. More than ____ requests from one person or family will be discussed in depth with the entire family."

"We expect advance notice of ____ (hours) (days) if children or grandchildren plan to visit."

"Children and grandchildren are welcome guests in our home for a period not to exceed _____."

"We have written down a list of house rules and the children/grandchildren *will* follow them. The list is posted in the _____."

There is no right or wrong plan when it comes to setting boundaries. Some couples like a total open door policy; flexibility to help the children and grandchildren out financially whenever they are in need. Others cannot live with that. But one common denominator exists: Make your policies and boundaries known to all members of your family. Be consistent. And, most importantly, don't be afraid to stand up to family members who fail to honor them.

Carl and Bess Warden's next door neighbors Bert and Meg Peterson found out the hard way about setting boundaries. Married almost forty years, Bert always had the upper hand in their relationship. He made all the decisions and Meg followed. "A proper wife of scripture," he called Meg. Carl called her a "doormat" and wondered if Meg was a truly happy woman.

This inequity came out when their grandson, William, wanted to live with them. He was attending a college located blocks away and wanted a rent-free living arrangement. His parents had already given him an ultimatum: "Earn your own keep. We're not supporting your student life-style anymore."

It seems William had changed majors five times in six years and obviously enjoyed the life of the professional student. His parents cut the moneybag strings. Now he needed to find another one.

At first Bert and Meg were flattered that their grandson wanted to live with them. Meg thought it would be great to have some help around the house, especially with the yard. Bert wasn't getting any younger and their extra large lawn was a chore for him to keep up with all the mowing, weeding, and clipping every week.

William moved in, but he never touched the lawn mower or even offered to help. Meg found she had one more mouth to feed, more clothes to wash, and another bed to make.

"Bert, you've got to talk to William. We can't go on this way," she complained one afternoon. Rocking the boat in any way was something she rarely did, but she was reaching the end of her rope. William was sponging off them, doubling her workload, and there sat Bert crowing about the perfect wife of scripture. Her resentment made her grit her teeth every time William walked through the door.

"Now, Meg, William's busy at school. It's the least we can do to help," Bert explained. William was, after all, his favorite grandson and a whiz at that. They had spent most of last evening in a very stimulating political discussion about the upcoming presidential election. Not to mention the Trivial Pursuit game that Bert managed to win by a hair, only because he lived most of the history questions William knew only academically.

Meg kept her mouth shut after that. Things continued to skid downhill even as her anger climbed. Only when she enlisted the help of her daughter and son-in-law (William's parents) did William finally move out. Bert resented Meg's lack of charity. Meg resented Bert. William had gone, but he left behind a sad rift.

With a lagging economy, it's not unusual for kids to be moving back in with parents or even grandparents. Sometimes it's either that or become homeless.

Boomerang Kids

That's the new term for kids who return home. The phenomenon is so common nowadays that many articles, books, and even comic strips, portray this new extended family living arrangement. "Pickles," a popular contemporary comic strip, features an elderly couple with their divorced daughter and her school-age son all living under the same roof. The variety and multitude of relationships in this family present lots of humorous material for the author.

In real life it's not so funny. Just when a couple is approaching retirement and looking forward to years to themselves, bang! The screen door slams and the kids say, "I'm home." The nest is full once again.

If a couple never accomplished the empty-nest task of the Fourth Passage, things will only get muddled and delayed further as the kids return again. If a couple did indeed fulfill the tasks of the Fourth Passage, they may find themselves saddled again with the trials of this Passage and even the Third when their children return.

It's a tricky balancing act and we don't have tried and true answers for every situation. Suffice it to say, though, that boundaries are extremely important in these situations. The returning children must have boundaries, the couple must have boundaries, and any grandchildren accompanying the children must have boundaries. And, everyone must be careful not to overstep those boundaries.

A joy to combat the problems of these returning children and grandchildren are the new relationships possible between grandparents and resident grandchildren. Again, the "Pickles" cartoon portrays this in the caring, humorous relationship between Grandpa and his grandson.

Even if the couple is not supporting their returning children and grandchildren, they may find themselves caring for the grandchildren while the children work or try to find work. In this age of dual working parents, couples who provide day-care for their grandchildren are becoming more and more common.

Well monitored and tempered, this day-care arrangement can actually be beneficial. It provides the grandparents with a well-deserved sense of need, youthfulness: an active mind and body. It gives the grandchildren a vital link with their roots, their past, and a wonderful insight into their parents. "This was Daddy when he was little? Wow!" Balance and comfort are the keys to making this arrangement work.

Day-care Grandparents

"It's great! Convenient. Nice," a woman named Margaret told us one afternoon in group counseling. "Mom takes care of Joey and Amy while I work. I don't know what we'd do without her."

"Does your mom say it's great, convenient, and nice?" we asked her.

Margaret's face went blank, as if the question should never have been asked by any sane person in the first place. "Mom adores Amy and Joey."

"Of course she does. Did she work when you were growing up?"

"No. She was home. A housewife."

"And now, thirty years later, after she's paid her dues and raised her children, she gets to sit at home. A housewife."

Margaret got a little testy. "Well, she's never complained about it. She'd complain if she didn't love to do it."

"Would she?"

The vast majority of grandparents do not complain. They feel guilty if they don't go along with extended visits, baby-sitting, live-in, and other arrangements. A nagging thought whispers, "Don't you love your grandchildren enough?"

Too, today's grandparents were raised in an atmosphere that required parents and grandparents to please others first and to make sacrifices silently. "Be nice. Do not make waves." They were taught to relegate their own needs, and especially their own wishes, to everyone else's needs and wishes. It was considered selfish to serve your own wants and needs, no matter how important they may be to you.

Unfortunately, despite the guilt and the desire to please, those "properly" trained grandparents do indeed resent having to constantly put their own wants and needs on hold. They did what God and society expected of them, making the postponements and sacrifices needed to get the kids raised and on their own. Now they are expected to do it all over again? Think again.

Besides, they're twenty or thirty years older. They may no longer have the strength and energy it takes to raise a second family.

They may no longer have the ready financial resources.

"I don't know how I raised three kids," an exhausted woman said. "I can't even keep up with one toddler grandson now. I know why God made it so that you can only have children when you're young."

Please understand we are not talking here about instances where grandparents watch their grandchildren while the parents take short vacations away.

"We're all for that!" Debi Newman agrees. "Parents need breaks to be together, to renew intimacy without that little knock on the bedroom door. Grandparents also need special times with their grandchildren. It's a win-win situation for all involved."

"My best memories of childhood," Brian Newman recalls, "are the times I spent with my grandfather."

By contrast, rather, we're talking here about the instances where the grandparents are providing regular, long-term child care for their grandchildren, many times without monetary compensation.

"Pay me? To watch my own grandchildren?! I wouldn't hear of it!"

It is an option we urge every boomerang family to consider. While you are considering it, think what day-care of the caliber the grandparents provide is worth on the open market, if you can find it at all.

There are situations when a grandparent is the only choice for a parent. It's either impose on the folks or go on welfare, starve, or go homeless. Also, some grandchildren have health conditions that preclude them from being in traditional day-care situations. In those instances, the grandparents may be the only option. That is a whole different ball game from the use of grandparents as a convenience.

Still, the same potential for conflict and resentment is there. We won't go into pages and pages of advice in this area. Situations are so individualized that generalizations won't help much. Rather, let us stress that if you are in a situation of providing day-care for your grandchildren, think carefully about the parameters around which you will provide this service. Look over the following list of thought-provokers. Make sure you and your spouse both answer these questions, separately. Then compare answers and, most importantly, talk it over.

"How long am I willing to commit to watch the grandchildren—days, weeks, months, years?"

"Who will be responsible for the food they will consume while I'm watching them?"

"Will I have time off for vacations, not dependent on their parents' vacation time?" "Who will shuttle the grandkids to their various school and extracurricular activities?"

"Do I want to receive compensation for watching the grandchildren while my daughter/son works?" (Be honest now!)

"Can I rely on standard hours of work? Will my son/ daughter drop off the kids and pick them up at decent hours each day?"

"Do I have the freedom to ask for an occasional day or hour off as I want it?"

And the most important questions of all:

"Do I really want to do this, or am I doing it for my son or daughter's sake?"

"What will we be giving up if we agree to watch the grandkids?"

May and Gary agonized over those questions above. Complicating their decision was the simple fact that Cody was so hyper and so difficult that baby-sitters rarely accepted him more than once. Could they themselves turn him around from monster to model? No. Only the parents could do that, and for a variety of reasons, they could not see that happening.

A further complication was their daughter's defensive attitude. More than once she threatened to break off all contact between Cody and his grandparents if they refused to help on her terms, or if they got nasty. (Her idea of nasty was a failure to take Cody when she wanted them to or to discipline Cody without her say-so. She was the parent and she would decide on matters of discipline.) She was wielding a hammer, of course. She was their daughter; she knew instinctively their weak spots.

May and Gary sought the advice of a counselor who specializes in geriatrics. The woman attended their church and they knew her socially. (Here's a good rule of thumb when you are confused about a course of action. Seek the advice of someone you trust. That's often hard for grandparent-ish people to do.)

The woman's advice: Draw up a contract and adhere to it.

May and Gary's objection: The daughter will break off all contact if we get tough.

The counselor's question: Whose welfare is most important?

The immediate answer: Cody's.

Are his interests served by the present arrangement?

No.

May and Gary sat their daughter and son-in-law down and showed them a written agreement based pretty much on the points in the exercise above. They paid particular attention to the matter of discipline. When they had Cody, they would discipline him their way. They showed the parents a calendar of events they planned to attend and places they intended to go. First on the calendar was a tour in a rented RV down to the coast and Padre Island. May and Gary had wanted to do that for years.

The daughter balked, and really didn't believe they meant what the contract and calendar said. It was a suggestion. They weren't going to get tough; they never had so far. A week later the following phone call ensued:

"Mom, you'll have to take Cody tomorrow. I have a dental appointment in the morning and that thing with the newspaper in the afternoon. The regular baby-sitter broke her arm this morning and can't take him."

"We're leaving for Brownsville tomorrow. I'm sorry."

"You can postpone it a day. A day won't hurt. And I'm desperate."

"I'm sorry."

Note that May avoided arguing or bantering. And in a fit of protocol she tactfully kept herself from saying "you're always desperate."

"Mom, you're not serious. Which is more important, your grandson, or a vacation you can take any time?"

"I'm sorry."

Again, even though the daughter immediately hit the guilt button, May avoided getting into a discussion. Her daughter did not ask *why?* But had she, May was prepared to say, "It's not open to discussion," over and over.

Was it easy? It killed her. May hated saying "I'm sorry." This felt so alien, so wrong, this putting one's own self first. May felt guilty for doing so, far guiltier than her daughter could make her. And their next step hurt even worse.

The daughter, never one to take "no" for an answer, arrived at the doorstep early the next morning anyway, Cody in tow. She discovered to her shock that May and Gary had left even earlier (four in the morning, to be precise, just so as not to be there if Cody showed up).

May's neighbor, a no-nonsense older lady, sat on the porch, tipping casually back and forth in her bentwood rocker. "They left for Brownsville," she announced. "Door's locked."

"What am I going to do?" the daughter wailed.

"Well, just this once, I'll watch Cody for you if you want. Only once, mind you. I've met him."

"Oh, would you? That's wonderful!"

"I charge fifteen dollars an hour."

"An *hour* . . . ?"

"Payable in advance."

The Joys

We've talked a lot about pitfalls and inconveniences—about negatives or near-negatives, as it were. But the positives outweigh negatives, especially where grandkids are concerned.

There are many different ways in which grandparents are a positive influence on grandchildren. You will recall at the beginning of the book, at the wedding of Carl and Bess Warden's granddaughter, Julia Karris said sadly, "Beth Anne is so lucky. My mom never attended my weddings—either one of them—let alone my grandparents." Her grandparents' support would have made an important difference in her life—not just at her wedding, of course, but throughout her life. Julia needed stability, wisdom, comfort, and strength many times during her life. Her grandparents could have helped provide them.

And then there's the little town in Oklahoma that bills itself as the world's friendliest. That little town boasts major community support of the school and the students, and the boast is not idle. Certainly no one there could imagine placing a limit on the number of friends and relatives who can attend a school function. The school auditorium, which holds a thousand, was pretty much filled at the June commencement exercises. The senior class numbered one hundred and seventeen.

"Would the parents of our seniors rise?" the superintendent asked the assemblage. More than two hundred persons rose. The seniors and guests applauded the parents.

"And would the grandparents please rise?" Well over two hundred others stood up. Some had sacrificed to come this night. A few had traveled several thousand miles for this moment. The seniors, all one hundred and seventeen of them, rose as one, turned, and gave their grandparents a spontaneous standing ovation.

That is what kids think of grandparents. Oh, sure, as they enter their teens, they complain how stodgy and old-fashioned those old folks are. They may even behave disrespectfully. They may not acknowledge your importance for years, perhaps not even in your lifetime. Rest assured—rest *very* assured—that your importance as a grandparent is paramount.

Grandkids are fun. You enjoy a sense of importance when the kids and grandkids need you, for baby-sitting or whatever. But the bottom line, the ultimate joy, is the satisfaction of knowing you are making a difference in their lives.

And always remember you are their link with their heritage.

"I have such a scant heritage, I know almost nothing about my ancestors," laments Brian Newman. "I feel that lack, and I want my children to have a better link with their past."

Perhaps that's why Brian is an antiques enthusiast. People made these old, old items. People used them. One of his prized antiques is a prayer bench, or kneeler, a prie-dieu. He doesn't use it for prayer much, though, at least when his preschooler Rachel is up. Rachel has adopted the prayer bench as her own, and prays at it nightly, after the bedtime story.

Brian put the word out among the antique dealers he knows, and obtained a second prie-dieu. The second one is for Benjamin, the baby. He is having brass plates prepared, with Rachel's and Benjamin's names and a few words about the significance of the kneelers. The kneelers are heirlooms for his children and his children's children. When one has no link from generation to generation, one must make do.

You, as the generation who remembers World War II firsthand, are the essential link to all our yesterdays.

Links and baby-sitters and mentors—all the roles older people fill that no one else can—are rarely easy roles. They are fulfilling, joyful, perhaps invigorating. But not easy.

It was immensely difficult for May and Gary to set new boundaries as they did, and infinitely more difficult to enforce them. It took several episodes and many trying moments before the adjustment could be called complete.

Cody still comes around, although the daughter was *very*

cool for six months or so. Cody isn't quite the blowtorch-in-a-munitions factory that he used to be. At least, when he's at his grandparents', he knows where the line is, although he rarely toes it willingly.

And that is one of the joys May and Gary have found. They can be a positive influence in their grandchild's life. May and Gary finally figured out that, essentially, grandchildren are not their responsibility. They learned that too much of a good thing can be bad. Most vitally, they learned the crucial importance of the Fifth Passage as a time to be together, the best and most solid time to renew intimacy with each other. They no longer let anyone or anything jeopardize that. They had earned their freedom with a lifetime of work. They deserved it.

You deserve it too.

Try one issue free...

That's right! We're so convinced that you will love **TODAY'S BETTER LIFE**, the full-color quarterly magazine from the experts at the Minirth-Meier Clinics, that we will send you an issue *absolutely free* when you return this card.

In it you'll find practical advice on improving your health, strengthening relationships, and growing in your faith. And all of the articles are written by experts committed to helping you grow stronger emotionally, physically, and spiritually.

Return this card or call our toll free number to start down the path to better life *today.*

☐ **YES,** I want to take advantage of this special offer for **TODAY'S BETTER LIFE**. Send me my free issue. If I like what I see, I'll pay only $16.95 for a one-year subscription. If not, I'll write "cancel" on the invoice and owe nothing.

NAME: _____

ADDRESS: _____

CITY: _____ STATE: _____ ZIP: _____

Or call toll free: 1-800-982-0500

- ■ BALANCE YOUR LIFE
- ■ DEEPEN YOUR FAITH
- ■ IMPROVE YOUR HEALTH

Please allow 4–6 weeks for your first issue to arrive. Offer good in U.S. only. Standard rate is $19.80 for four issues.

EBW02-2

BUSINESS REPLY MAIL
FIRST CLASS MAIL PERMIT NO. 619, MARION, OH

POSTAGE WILL BE PAID BY ADDRESSEE

BETTER LIFE

P.O. Box 1924

Marion, OH 43306-2024

Chapter 5

Can You Renew Intimacy?

W ynn and Maggie had been married forty-two years. After retirement, Wynn worked part-time as a night handyman at a nearby nursing home. When something blew up at 2 A.M., they'd call him and he'd fix it somehow. He was good at his job. But a mild stroke reduced his physical strength in one side and put a reluctant end to his part-time job, and Wynn quit trying.

Maggie had always been a "Nervous Nellie," bustling about, tending to Wynn's needs, keeping the house. But there is a factor called "polarization" that affects every marriage that negatively influenced Maggie and Wynn's union. Polarization makes the couple's normal tendencies become more pronounced. If she is an early riser and he a late one, she will rise ever earlier, ever brighter, and he will slug in the bed ever longer. If he is dominant and she reticent, he will become more dominant. If they switch roles for any reason (dominance is a good example), the switch will become ever more pronounced. If she becomes dominant she will do so exceedingly.

Now, thanks to polarization, Maggie bustled all the more. She even cleaned his glasses and cut his meat for him. His horizons ended at sports on TV, and he went to sleep during the games.

Doctors assigned Wynn exercises to help him become more self-sufficient and build his stamina. Wynn ducked them. He learned quickly that if he pedaled his stationary bike real hard for fifteen seconds, he could lift his feet away from the pedals and coast, putting a good half mile on the odometer with no effort at all. Maggie hit the roof when she found out.

Wynn had closed down his world around himself. Unfortunately, he dragged Maggie's horizons in as well. When he suffered a second stroke and needed a walker to get around the house, Maggie tied herself to him completely, afraid he might try to move around and fall. She wouldn't go out and sit on the front porch if Wynn stayed in the house, and Wynn rarely went out on the porch. Wynn became too heavy a burden for her, of course, for he did fall, often pulling her down with him. He spent his last years in the nursing home where he had once served as night handyman.

So often, in counseling and amid friendships, we see people eyeing the bad as they grow older, hardly ever looking around for the "something good" of later life. Good-byes are coming thick and fast at this stage of life. But good-byes are not so much an end as a beginning. By severing one connection, a good-bye frees you to accept a new connection. Good-byes are more than balanced by hellos. Both will profoundly influence your marriage. "Grow old along with me," invited Robert Browning. "The best is yet to be."

We invite you to look upon the changes in this Fifth Passage as another network of good-byes and hellos, of something good linked to the bad. While this is a handy way to look at life in general, and your marriage in particular, during any passage, now in these latter days is when the philosophy pays rich dividends. Here, too, is a splendid opportunity to deepen intimacy, as you and your mate explore these hellos and good-byes and talk about them together.

Fighting the Image

It's not just younger people who entertain false attitudes toward the aging.

*   "Set in their ways."
*   "Persnickety."
*   "Slow. You see a line of cars and you can just bet that the car in front holding everybody up is an old person."
*   "Cranky."
*   "They don't tip worth beans. I hate having to wait on them in the restaurant."

Ours is one of the very few cultures in the world that does not honor, even revere, the aged. When Corrie Ten Boom, the Dutch woman who spent terrifying years in a Nazi concentration camp for hiding Jews during World War II, traveled into southeast Asia, she was referred to most affectionately as "double-old grandmother," a term of reverence, of extreme respect. Here that would be an insult.

Many Fifth Passage couples enjoy the fruits of a slower lifestyle.

They either ignore or put up with relationship issues that used to irritate them.

And many younger people, looking at the decelerated pace of older couples, don't understand. They see this winding down as giving in to boredom. In a way it is, perhaps, but that's not necessarily negative. There is much to be said for feeling at ease with life.

These later years become a real time of contentment and that is much of their purpose. Younger people must come to grasp that. Says Brian Newman, "Until I visited Dad not too long ago, I never sat on our back porch and watched the birds. It was a great experience."

Younger people also tend to condemn the revisionist history older people so often indulge.

"Remember when we played ball?"

"Dad, we never played ball."

"Oh, come on! Don't you remember when?"

"You were always working. You were never there."

For couples in the Fifth Passage, this revised history serves a special purpose. The couples may be using it to deal with disappointment and personal guilt. By romanticizing aspects of the past (to the point of hallucinating, the kids claim), they find a special means of making peace with painful memories. They cannot go back and change the past literally, so they do it mentally. We caution younger people against a militant confrontation of their elders to no good end. In this stage, moderate revisions of remembrances serve some positive value.

As one ages, one forgets the bad and ugly, but again that's not necessarily a negative thing. Positive memories have a powerful influence, whether they reflect the lock step of fact or embellish it a bit.

Grandkids idolize grandparents, and that can also cause problems, believe it or not, because the parents of the grandkids too often do not. As Bill Cosby says, "You didn't know them when." The children know what those parents were like. If their memories are sour, they have a hard time watching their own children accept the grandparents so freely.

Kathy loved her grandparents. She never understood why her mother despised them. Kathy learned to live a separate life with her grandparents. She visited and helped them as a young adult, but she rarely mentioned them when speaking to her mother. When her mother would ask her where she had been, rather than tell her mother she had been with her grandparents, she often made excuses.

Kathy's mother never resolved her anger with Kathy's grandparents. And she resented Kathy for loving and admiring them.

Kathy's grandparents may have been different people as she

was growing up than they were when they were raising her mother. She can never know those people as they were back then. They've changed. But her mother cannot see them in the same light Kathy does because her perception is so colored by the past.

What others think is secondary. What is important: do those persons, married well over three decades, accept the negative stereotypes or do they maintain a strong faith in themselves? What do they think of each other?

If the partners themselves begin believing some of the problem images, they can drift apart by making wrong assumptions. We saw the seed of that in the Fourth Passage, when too often the partners made untrue cultural assumptions about sexual needs and desires.

Some of those assumptions could be framed in statements such as these:

- "She's had her change of life, so she's not interested in sex anymore."
- "My husband is over fifty, so of course he's going to start folding in the middle."
- "Old people don't appreciate sex."

These assumptions and others could be alleviated at least in part by talking to each other. Talking to each other means growing—growing in understanding of each other, in appreciation of each other, in tolerance for each other. And if the partners' marriage has been growing, these latter years usher in a beautiful season of peace. If the partners are frozen up in an earlier passage, unable to mature, the strife multiplies.

The second task of the Fifth Passage leads to a peaceful coexistence during these later years: Continue renewing your love despite the many cultural pressures and family myths that push in the opposite direction.

The Second Task: Continue Renewing Love

Powerful deterrents block completion of this task. Plain old stagnation often becomes a major culprit hindering revitalization of your love. It's so easy to drift, to close into oneself, to do the same familiar thing, to take all the usual stuff (and that includes the spouse) for granted. Indeed, many older people mistake stagnation for peace.

Wynn and Maggie had stagnated. Were you to ask him, Wynn would say he was at peace. What he was, was out of it. Part of the problem was his stroke. But the most of it was his neglect to do anything stimulating, or even to keep up with life. Vegetating (vegging out, the kids call it) is not peace.

Maggie in her frenetic do-everything mode, would claim honestly that she knew no peace. Her constant activity, however, was nothing close to growth. She did her busywork in the same ways, following the same rote patterns, preparing the same meals (delicious meals; not a thing wrong with the cooking!), and following the same routes to the same stores. She watched the news at night because everyone watches the news and she wanted to sit awhile after she cleaned up the kitchen.

She rarely spoke to Wynn or he to her. When they did speak, it concerned surface things.

"Did you see that guy on TV who milks rattlesnakes?"

"Uh-huh."

"Time for your pills. You want water or milk?"

"Water."

Maggie took exquisite care of Wynn. And down inside she resented it exquisitely, something she would not admit aloud, not even to herself. The two of them together contributed nothing whatever to the growth of intimacy in their marriage. What does not grow dies.

People who stagnate quit growing. For all the action, Maggie, for example, experienced no personal growth. Stagnating people don't check books out of the library anymore. They never get out to see new things or open the door to new ideas. They don't talk much to each other, and when they do it's usually to check the broadcast time of that favorite syndicated game show. Physical deterioration encourages and compounds stagnation. We see among our friends, and in the clinic, persons who so gave up on life they died emotionally years before death took them physically.

Antagonism also works against completion of this task. Picture this scene: Grant's sister is going to take elderly Grant and Edna out for a drive. Grant and Edna will be sitting in back. Grant opens the door for Edna. Before he can buck the seatback forward for her, Edna plops down into the front seat. Furious that he must now walk clear around the car to the other door, Grant mutters obscenities at his wife of forty-three years. Half-deaf, oblivious old Edna riffles through her purse, blissfully unaware of the bitterness and anger. Within a few minutes she will snap and swear at him just as viciously. When Edna dies two years later, Grant literally falls apart, unable to face life without the dotty old lady he so openly despised.

This antagonism that develops between couples who have not completed previous tasks and passages is not necessarily the opposite of love. People genuinely in love and people codependently enmeshed both may become intensely antagonistic of their mates.

Little annoyances grow into major grievances. Little habits become burs beneath saddles. Lack of growth in one partner brings disrespect from the other; conversely, growth in one can make insecure the one not growing any more.

By this stage, fortunately, the couple also has a lot going to help advance the task. Their long history together forms a powerful bond. Too, times change rapidly, and here is a couple who can collectively remember a lot of "ancient" history. Those memories separate and elevate them from the younger generations to whom the word "Hitler" is part of that ancient history. "Remember what we were doing when Hitler invaded Poland?" "Yeah, and we were living on one hundred dollars a month then—comfortably!" Ah, history.

One of the deterrents to completion of this second task is what we call, "Fifth Passage codependency." By codependency we mean a relationship where the boundaries of togetherness and separateness are not well-established. Younger people sensitive to codependency issues see codependency blossom in aging couples. Indeed, older people may see it in themselves, for the Fifth Passage is an easy place for a codependent relationship to develop or intensify.

Friends disappear. The kids are gone. Should one of the couple fall into ill health, as Wynn did, they soon find themselves locked in a particularly virulent codependency.

Fifth Passage Codependency

Wynn and Maggie failed this second task of the Fifth Passage miserably. It tripped Wynn and very nearly unhorsed Maggie in the end. Wynn had let his horizons close in. He had worked his whole life. Now was the time to kick back and relax: watch TV, sleep, vegetate.

Maggie didn't want to, but she let Wynn drag her into his closing world. She yearned to get out and do something, anything. She didn't, because of Wynn. Her response was not love. It was enmeshment.

What's the difference? Love does what's best for both partners. Love serves the highest needs—stimulation, health. Once Wynn began to fail, the two became almost totally codependently enmeshed in each other. Wynn let Maggie do everything; she refused to leave his side for a moment. (There's that polarization again, you see.) When Wynn entered the nursing facility, Maggie spent months in an intense depression, blaming herself for putting her husband out of his own home. Her head saw that she was too old to physically handle him anymore, but her heart did not. Her heart still loaded up on shame and guilt. She could not see how much he contributed to the situation by giving up. She only blamed

herself. If only she had worked harder. If only she had . . .
All of the messages she was giving herself were codependency
speaking.

Over and over in our practice we see that persons with
flawed love—people codependently enmeshed rather than en-
joying Transcendent Love—cannot envision life beyond the
death of a spouse. When one partner dies, the other may
frequently follow within one to two years.

When debilitation occurs, husband and wife tend to slip
into a codependent parent-child relationship unless both
guard against it. That is, the "child" becomes dependent
upon the "parent" for things the child could do alone if
forced to, and the "parent" becomes codependent on the
"child" in a desperate grasp at feeling needed, useful, necessary. When the "child" dies or enters institutional care, the
"parent" is devastated. Should the "parent" die or be dis-
abled, the "child" suffers as would an actual orphaned child.

Only a union of equals makes life as good as it can be right
up to the end. Only a solid peer relationship, maintained to
the end, assures that the surviving partner will make it past
the end with a minimum of pain.

The Positive Side of Fifth Passage Codependency

"A positive side of codependency?" you ask. Yes. Passage Five
can be a healthy and natural time of growing mutual interde-
pendence. Provided that the codependency does not get too
far out of hand, there are good points to it. Each partner gives
the other a renewed purpose for living. Each has something
to do, someone to take care of. The negative: When one
spouse dies, the other loses that purpose in life.

Another positive: Both realize that they're not a burden on
the kids (almost always a heavy concern). And their needs can
still be met by each other. They can capture, possibly for the
first time, a sense of unity, of togetherness.

Each Other's Life Support

In this Fifth Passage there are a lot of things you can get away with that would be labeled "unhealthy" or "codependent" or "dysfunctional" ten years ago. Many of these things improve intimacy if done with a loving heart. Nothing exotic, they are the practical things you may not think of as gifts. They are gifts.

Consider some of these:

_____ Monitoring your partner's health, medication, etc. (but please, no nagging. Okay?)

_____ Helping with movement out and about.

"I saw the most touching thing," relates Susan Hemfelt. "At a gas station a man was helping a woman, I presume his wife. He carried her into the rest room, then carried her out. She was just a frail little thing."

Back in the hills behind town, in a small hamlet, lives a woman with Parkinson's disease. When her husband sits around, usually at the table in the small dining alcove, he makes certain he is always within earshot of his wife. For he has to carry her upstairs to the bedroom, and when she is upstairs, downstairs to the bathroom. He does so without resentment or irritation. "Once I saw an elevator that you can install on stairs," he mused one day to a caseworker. "If'n I could do that, she could go upstairs without my help. She'd feel free."

_____ Cutting meat, helping with manual jobs.

_____ Reading aloud to a person with deteriorating eyesight.

_____ Practical nursing jobs that ten years ago would be totally inappropriate.

Consider the poignant scene toward the end of the film *Driving Miss Daisy*. The Jessica Tandy character lives in a nursing home, and her chauffeur, the Morgan Freeman character, comes to visit.

Her hand too shaky to manage a fork, he feeds her pie. A beautiful scene, and so very telling.

All these situations, and others like them, suggest dysfunction because they attempt to impose person A's control upon person B's actions, actions that should not and indeed cannot be controlled by A. Taken to extreme, and offered with resentment or rancor, A's attempts to control B spell trouble. Given in love, with a sense of being useful and helpful and needed, they can help marital intimacy grow.

Codependent dysfunctions are not the only deterrent to the renewal of love in this latter passage. So is isolation.

Isolation

Since her husband's death fifteen years ago, Liz has been living in her two-story family home alone. She no longer attends to the yard and garden. In fact, she no longer leaves the house at all.

Her son in nearby Plainfield visits her regularly. He takes care of routine maintenance and brings her groceries. When she answers the door to him she does not say, "It's good to see you, Phil!" She says, "Why are *you* here?" Phil is an intrusion on Liz's life and, quite frankly, at age eighty-seven, she can't see the use of him.

Liz's mother isolated herself similarly, and was cared for by Liz's brother until her death at ninety-two. Liz conveniently has forgotten her brother's burning rhetoric as he denounced the old woman who had made him her slave. For Liz is doing just that same thing to her son.

Voluntary isolation, in which the person methodically and progressively cuts off friends, relations, and outside contacts, runs epidemic in the Fifth Passage of marriage. A married couple becomes withdrawn, not just from the world but from each other too. They stop connecting and become introspective.

We believe several things are going on in this scenario. Surrounded by painful realities, persons prefer the numbness of depression to facing the pain. Remember how we spoke of this tendency in Chapter 3 on the grieving process? It's particularly prevalent in the Fifth Passage.

People having trouble in Passage Five, feeling a fear of leaving and of being left, will start shutting down the connections they previously had. They pursue the false belief that by severing themselves from all they hold dear, they won't get hurt when they lose it all. Isolation leads to its own depression and its own pain. It's an end run around the paradox of embracing, then releasing, life in order to enjoy it to the fullest.

Self-Blame

Some people go through life getting blamed. Not a few probably deserve it, though possibly what they are guilty of and what they get blamed for are two different things. Most, though, scarcely deserve the blame and invective they heap upon themselves. Many accept that blame for codependent reasons based in low self-esteem. As these persons enter the Fifth Passage, and the stakes are raised, they enter a period of deep depression and self-castigation. They feel, we think, that if somehow they devalue themselves enough, and blame themselves enough, they don't have to expect anything good or lasting from life.

We find this mind-set often in people who feel powerless about their lives. For example, teenagers, feeling powerless, engage in massive self-blame and self-destructive acts, drugs, alcohol, reckless driving, and sexual acting-out. So, too, the elderly bask in self-blame, and they may be even more powerless than teens.

For forty-two years, Joyce lived with a domineering, abusive man. She tolerated it in the prior passages because she could busy herself with the kids, with the house, with their small business. She didn't have to dwell on her own frustration and unhappiness, and, most importantly, she didn't have to work the problem out. When her loud, pushy husband announced to her that she was to blame for this difficulty and that difficulty, she accepted it. Why fight it? Now here they were in the final passage of their marriage, both of them frightened, panicked by what they saw coming. Life had been lousy and now it was over. The only thing Joyce knew to do was put herself down further.

Needless to say, self-blame also leads to depression. As we talked to Joyce we saw her self-blame as a way for her to squash any spark of hope that life might be better, or that the end of life is a celebration of all she had. "What nonsense!" she would be the first to say. Depression is the most widespread problem among people in their Fifth Passage. It is the great emotional health epidemic. Tellingly, depression is also rife among teens, the other powerless group.

Gerontologists are starting to say that one-third to one-half of what is seen as dementia (a technical term for loss of brain capacity), senility, or early Alzheimer's may be misdiagnosed depression. Sleeping all the time, being unable to think or to concentrate—these are depression symptoms, as well as symptoms of aging problems. The person evidencing those symptoms is often treated like a child. That makes the person more depressed, destroying self-esteem, and that makes the depression worse yet, in turn making the symptoms worse . . . and the spiral descends until the person is considered too feebleminded to function.

Be alert to the fact that depression can be exacerbated by several drugs routinely prescribed for blood pressure and heart problems. But be careful. A dose that is therapeutic in a person age sixty-five can be toxic to one seventy-five. Metabolism changes with age, and so, therefore, does drug tolerance. Toxicity can cause depression. We caution you to monitor medications very closely and to consult frequently with your physician about dosage and side effects. Adequate vigilance in this regard at sixty may not be adequate at seventy or

eighty. Check and recheck with a doctor experienced in ger-
ontology. Check also for contraindications; that is, the effects
two or more drugs have when they're mixed together in the
system. A heart medication is good. An allergy medication is
good. But what do they do together?

The final deterrent to renewing intimacy is blaming your
spouse for everything and anything.

Blame the Spouse

And why not? After all, the spouse has been with you all this
time, and is sitting right there, ripe to receive your castiga-
tion.

Instead of making peace with losses and changes of your
life, it is so much easier to just get stuck in the first step of the
grief process, shock and denial—anger turned outward—and
fire that anger at the nearest target. It's the opposite of self-
blame, and it does about the same thing. "It's your fault we
never have enough money." "It's your fault the kids never
come visit anymore." "It's your fault I have heart problems."

"That," claims Dr. Minirth, "is projection, pure and simple. The person who doesn't want to face some reality inside
the self projects it onto another person. He's getting rid of it,
you see. Projection is an effective, albeit twisted, way of handling any problems. Instead of working the problem out in-
ternally, you simply dump it externally onto your partner."

We find that factors in people's lives predisposing them to
this dumping were at work in them from the beginning of
their marriage.

Through prior passages, this projection simmered and it
was tolerable. Now that real problems loom—death and dis-
ability—the coping mechanism escalates into something ex-
plosive. Too, the couple was distracted in prior passages as
they struggled to raise the kids, buy the house or set up the
retirement plan, juggle the career, and marry the children off.

The person not willing to go through all the grief steps we
mentioned in Chapter 3—personally resolving the pain, suf-

fering through to resolution; can duck the pain in one of two ways: get stuck in a grief step and refuse to go on, or project everything onto the spouse.

Rarely is projection displayed as dramatically as a recent case in the newspapers. A minister was counseling an elderly couple when the man pulled out a gun and shot his wife. Projection is usually more subtle. But what went on below the conscious level of that man's mind bears scrutiny. His survival method, his way of dodging death, was to lay all blame on his wife. Then, symbolically, like a true scapegoat or animal sacrifice, she could carry it away into death. Through her he seemingly got rid of it all.

We meet many people in Passage Five who do the same thing without the gun. A woman announces to her spouse on the eve of their fortieth anniversary, "I'm divorcing you." She is killing off the other person symbolically. A man or woman may burn with such anger that he or she blocks the spouse out completely—another symbolic death.

Usually, a person blaming another excessively will, at some level, feel a lot of self-imposed guilt. It's probably a mix of true guilt and false guilt. Instead of grieving through that, sifting out false guilt from that which is authentic, the person turns it all into anger and dumps it on someone else to get rid of it.

We've looked at the deterrents to renewing love. Daunting, at times, those deterrents. Now let's answer that all-important question: *Is it worth investing any further intimacy in this union? It's all going to be gone soon anyway.*

The Intimacy Investment

Mary Alice Minirth has already thought out her answer to that all-important question: "Persons on their deathbed don't ask for their banker or interior decorator or old boss from work. They want their spouse: their best friend. I watched my dad do that."

People in extremity want the company of persons with whom they have developed intimate relationships. Not economic or vocational or even medical relationships. Investment in intimacy offers rich returns when the chips are down.

But when relationships as well as people grow old, when to renew intimacy seems old hat, not to mention a bother, when the sexual aspect of intimacy is grinding to a halt, how does one dream again the old dream? How does one build intimacy at this late stage of the game?

Brian Newman's grandfather commented to Debi about her grandmother-in-law, "I still think she's as pretty as she was at sixteen." They were well into their seventies.

Blindness? No. Appreciation. He saw delicate, translucent skin, not wrinkles; he looked at her form and recalled the allure she had always held for him. He didn't see as a camera sees; history was shaping his vision.

You do the same thing with your flower beds. What do you see in your flower beds on a winter day? Your eyes see a few brown stalks, the grave markers of beauty long dead. But your memory sees the columbines and dahlias that will grow there six months from now.

When you admire a rose bush in bloom you see a glorious cascade of color, despite that over ninety percent of the actual two-dimensional plant surface meeting your eyes is foliage. Your eye skips over the foliage to focus on the flowers, minimizing the green and maximizing the color. Brian's grandfather was being honest. He saw what had been and what was still there; he did not bother seeing the ravages of age. He was not in denial; he was simply seeing beyond the eyes, for true vision sees beyond the physical image. That's appreciation.

Sexual Intimacy

Sex at seventy? Eighty? Some wink and dismiss the thought immediately. Others know better. As couples enter the Fifth Passage of marriage sexual interest gradually declines, but rarely disappears entirely, even in the oldest of the old. Most often the decline in frequency of intercourse is due to male sexual dysfunction, usually erectile failure, which is either a normal part of the aging process or the result of disease. Because there is a gradual decline in the conduction velocity of the penile nerves, greater stimulation is required. As a result of this, and the fact that blood circulation to the penis is less, the elderly man's penis takes longer to become erect, is less rigid, and remains erect for a shorter period of time.

Yet Passage Five can be an opportunity for sexuality rather than a time to abandon it.

Sometimes, for instance, you may improve an aging couple's sex life by reassuring the male partner of his capacity to perform.

That's one conclusion drawn from a study of thirty-two married couples, age fifty to seventy-seven, in which the husband had undergone prostate surgery. If the man believed his sexual function was unimpaired he had fewer problems with arousal and orgasm.

Another positive factor can be the importance of relationships at this time of life.

At the clinic we often tell parents that relationships are everything to young children. Don't worry about material gifts.

Don't fret that your child might see imperfection. Build a relationship. That's all the child needs. As we mature, material objects and financial security became, for the most part, just a little too important. Toys for boys. Upwardly mobile. Now in the Fifth Passage we come full circle again. Couples begin to reorder their priorities. Relationships again take ascendancy. Not the mortgage. Not even the bank account. Not the membership in the country club. All of that pales in comparison to relationships with other human beings and with God.

Since relationships are everything and since sexuality allows us to better experience a sense of union with another person, your spouse, sexuality in Passage Five can, in fact, be deeper than ever before. Sex in Passage Two, for instance, sometimes has specific goals, like procreating the next generation and relieving tension.

"Nothing cures a bad day like good sex" the young man claims. Now in Passage Five, these two purposes slip away. The emphasis is on union and the joy of that experience.

Couples also have better opportunity for appreciating the interrelationship between sexuality and spirituality, since people of this age are generally more attuned to the spiritual than younger people. Experts have long said that there is a special interrelationship between these two, rather than a dichotomy. Sexuality and spirituality can be mutually reinforcing.

We believe that sexual intercourse is much more than a biological or physiological function. In the marriage relationship, sex can be a sacrament. During the sexual experience we are able to participate momentarily in a symbolic way in a special type of spiritual union. For example people tell us they feel

- a sense of ecstatic surrender and yielding
- a feeling that time is standing still
- a special sense of bliss
- a sense of empowerment
- and finally a sense of transcendent union during the sexual experience—all emotions of the spiritual experience

Stop a moment and consider your own attitudes about sexuality in this passage of life. Does your mind tell you, I can't or shouldn't be sexual in Passage Five? If so, think of the roadblocks to sexuality—the messages from our culture, from the church, from your family-of-origin, and from this marriage—that might be influencing you.

From Our Culture

All of us have seen the cartoons in magazines and newspapers that portray sexual intimacy at this stage of life as humorous.

Such jokes build a bias within us that says, "Sex after sixty is a no-no."

We all derive from interesting cultures, and all are different. Think about the environment, the culture that has surrounded you in youth and now. What cultural biases can you think of that are affecting you? Look for jokes and adages as well as specific statements.

_____

_____

Now think about rewriting those biases into new endorsements for Passage Five sexuality. *(For instance you might affirm, "Such cartoons are ludicrous. Sexuality is valuable and important in these years.")*

_____

_____

Culture does not just dictate attitudes about the sexuality of older persons, but the sexuality of anyone. Can an old message of "Sex is naughty. Sex is bad." still haunt a couple who have been engaged in marital relations for well over three decades? It sure can. Unless quelled, those messages persist over the whole lifetime. And people who grew up in the thirties, forties, and fifties got that message in megadoses.

"I (can) (cannot) list three avenues through which I could have received the message 'sex is wrong.' "

_____

_____

"Here are three ways in which I can reassure myself and my spouse that sex inside the marriage bond is God-given and appropriate:"

_____

_____

_____

From the Church

One couple came to us after the husband had undergone urinary tract surgery. The doctor told him that sex was still possible; it would just take a little time and effort to retrain the nerve pathways. His wife rejected the idea so they decided to counsel with their minister. "This is a time when we are to put down our sexuality," the minister told them, "and lift God up."

A couple who accepts this minister's underlying premise— that sexuality will inhibit our ability to reconcile with God—is put in a real dilemma during this passage. Spirituality or sexuality—never both? Let us say it again: we believe that the two are interrelated rather than dichotomous.

Have you heard statements or inferences about sex-after-sixty in a church setting—the pastor's message, for example, or a Sunday school class? Mention them below:

_____

_____

Now think about rewriting them into endorsements of sex at seventy. *(For instance, "I know (or will look for) couples in the church who can be role models to me. Their sexual relationship encourages us to sustain our sexuality.")*

_____

_____

From Your Family-of-Origin

We pick up pounds and pounds of attitudes about geriatric sex from Mom and Dad. If they moved to separate bedrooms in their sixties, the message about sex rings out loud and clear.

Think about your parents' lives together, and what they said—intimations and jokes as well as pronouncements. What messages specifically did your parents pass along to you?

_____

_____

Now consider revising these messages with new endorsements, such as "I have chosen to reject my parents' model. My spouse and I shall remain physically close in the same bedroom for the rest of our years or as long as this is possible."

_____

_____

From This Marriage

The man who wanted to reestablish sexual intimacy with his wife after his surgery was bumping into his wife's inhibitions.

Is there some resistance in your marriage?

_____

_____

Consider confronting your spouse with new endorsements for sexuality. (For instance, "I love you and me and our marriage enough that I will continue to reinvite you to move back into a sexual union, not because I want to control you but as an expression of my love for you and our marriage.") Such an endorsement or statement might be: _____

_____

_____

Chances are 50 percent that you are the one inhibited in some way. Think of what your spouse has said to you in the past that might indicate this is so. Think about what you know of good sex from healthy sex education. Are these pictures a picture of your own sex life? While remaining aware of the easy way projection can occur, examine your own sexual biases and inhibitions. Detail them if you like: _____

_____

_____

If You Could Change

When Wynn gave up, he gave up. He didn't even try to perform lovemaking, and going into the nursing home sealed it for sure.

"Use it or lose it" applies to sexual activity at this age. And yet, should a man and woman of advanced age marry anew, they very frequently find they can bring back the magic.

Too, we've found that couples in the Fifth Passage can have an unusual perspective toward sex. Their sexual relationship can go either way. If good sexual channels are open (if there is no real physical impediment to sex), this experience can be deeper than ever. If, however, illness makes sex impossible, spouses have a better capacity to accommodate that situation.

A true paradox exists here. At this time when we are nearing the end of our story, we can feel greater sexual fulfillment rather than the leftovers, as some would have us believe.

Some of the changes inherent in aging are actually for the better. In the man, the nerves serving his primary sexual organs do not fire as strongly as they did twenty years ago. He will require more stimulation to reach erection. Because his blood circulation is somewhat reduced (for one reason, because of restricting arteries, or "hardening of the arteries," the same cause that brings on heart attacks), the erection will not be as firm nor sustained as long. Indeed, it may come and go. He may be taking medications that seriously reduce his capabilities. (Ask your doctor about that specifically; inquire regarding every drug you take.)

For the woman's part, she will be slower to produce lubricant and the volume of lubricant is reduced somewhat. She will be a little slower achieving orgasm. She will benefit greatly from lengthier foreplay.

Ah, but you see the value of that? It is normal for both partners to enjoy extended foreplay. Earlier in life, sex was, well, it was hastier. Now it can be enjoyed at leisure, literally, with involved foreplay, more "messing around," more attention to the activity itself. The sexual union takes longer to achieve, but it is much sweeter, and surprisingly more satisfying.

Many men in later years learn by experiment that they can sustain erection, and achieve a better orgasm, in some sexual positions more than in others. This is a purely mechanical phenomenon. Blood engorges the penis because of an intricate system of vessels and dams. If any of them are damaged or weakened, engorgement is reduced. By changing position relative to gravity, the man partially compensates for the damage or weakening. The end result is that a man who does not function to his own satisfaction in one position may find himself doing just fine in another.

If you could change something about your normal, everyday sexual experience, what would it be (techniques, time of day, positions, surroundings . . .)? _____

_____

_____

What has your spouse indicated that he or she would like to try, alter, or improve? _____

_____

_____

Now sit down with your spouse and discuss the above two exercises. The discussion may or may not lead to changes, but the primary goal of the discussion is not change per se. The primary goal is the discussion itself.

Communion

Another breeding ground of intimacy: simply sitting down and talking to each other. There are important topics to be discussed in this passage. When will you transmit your material and financial legacies to the next generations? Have you both agreed to the provisions of a will? Is it up to date? What family history do you want to make certain the next generation knows? How have you arranged for its transmission? Explore each other's thoughts.

"We've been building intimacy for half a century," the old man complains. "Aren't we there yet?"

Remember we've been talking about growth, as well. Young people can hardly avoid growing. Older people can keep growing. Growth means change. What was true of your partner last week or even yesterday may not be true anymore. Or the truth may have shifted. Intimacy means knowing your partner now. As growth changes the two of you, continuing intimacy keeps both of you caught up on the differences.

Improved intimacy is, in many ways, a form of growth itself.

Horizons

Maggie sat in a little cafe by the city park, watching kids feed popcorn to the ducks. "I thought my world ended when Wynn went into the home," she said to us. "It took me about six months to emerge from the cloud I had wrapped around me. It was a wrenching good-bye." She smiled. "You were talking about good-byes being the opened doors to hellos. It was. My life has been one hello after another lately."

Maggie visits Wynn daily. She brings him treats and talks to him. She shares all the mail. But she has shoved her horizons back out, far beyond the old limits. It was hard at first. The easiest thing is to give up and let the world close in. Maggie had to fight that.

She attended a caning workshop to learn the craft and re-caned the seats of those four old chairs that had been hanging up in the attic. "They turned out beautifully," she purred. Now she's weaving new seats for her son-in-law's wood-canvas canoe.

At first, Maggie had to make herself join others for lunch somewhere, or invite old family friend Mrs. Smits over for dinner. These days, though, she looks forward to it. "Do you know what that Smits did?" she fumed. (She never referred to Mrs. Smits simply as Smits. It was *that* Smits.) "I made pig stomach and invited—"

"Pig stomach?" we asked cautiously.

"We used to stuff a real pig stomach, back when we butchered. I don't use a stomach; I just make up the sausage with celery and potatoes and onions without the stomach part. But we still call it pig stomach.

"I invited that Smits over and then I was going to take some up to the home for Wynn. Smits asked if she could have some of the leftover for lunch, and didn't she pop out a plastic box and take almost the whole thing! So I had to make more to take up to Wynn."

Maggie's disgust was tinged with a smile in the corner of her mouth. Her pig stomach was still the best in the county and worth fighting over.

Check Out Your Horizons

Assuming that you are entering your Fifth Passage, or approaching it—it's never too early to expand your horizons— how are your horizons doing? Check the statements below that apply to you:

_____ "There is one skill (like Maggie's cooking)—or more— that I can do better than anyone else around. It is (they are):

_____

_____ ."

_____ "My spouse can say the same: _____

_____ ."

_____ "I have at least one new skill or craft at my command that I didn't know how to do five years ago. It is:

_____

_____ ."

_____ "My spouse can say the same: _____

_____ ."

_____ "If I needed a friend this minute I could call any of three people. They are: _____

_____

_____ ."

_____ "My spouse has three also. They are: _____

_____

_____ ."

_____ "My spouse and I know the three best places—restaurants or cafes—within a twenty-mile radius to eat lunch. They are: _____

_____

_____ ."

_____ "We know two excellent little places to buy a good breakfast. They are: _____

_____ ."

_____ "We have seen at least one Academy-Award-nominated film in the last year. It was: _____

_____ ."
_____ "I (agree) (disagree) with the nominating committee."

_____ "My spouse and/or I each have our own library cards. The best book I've checked out in the last month is: _____ Because: _____

_____

_____ ."

Friendships

We covered the importance of friends in detail in *Renewing Love* (Nashville: Thomas Nelson, 1993), our book on the Fourth Passage of marriage. Perhaps even more critical in this passage, we advise couples to continue to foster friendships. You can have an intimate relationship with other people than your spouse now. There's a future benefit to this. One day you may no longer have your spouse. Then, there will just be your friends. Make sure you have surrounded yourself with people who care.

The only good way to do so is to be a person who cares. You've often heard the old saw, "To have a friend, be one." Never was it more true than now.

Liz, whom we described in the section on isolation, once enjoyed a lovely halo of good friends. In the past, she was active in her area's garden club. They gave her recognition awards in gratitude for her long work. She belonged to the women's auxiliary of her husband's lodge. She and her husband contributed time and money to several service organizations. She was active in her church.

What will Liz do if her son Phil is hit by a truck tomorrow? She will certainly be unable to handle such simple get-out-of-the-house things as grocery shopping, banking, mailing a parcel at the post office. The day is coming when she will no longer be able to negotiate the stairs in her house and must move to a one-story residence. However in the world will she find one?

From the vast assortment of acquaintances she had, few would have qualified as friends. But she would have had those few. They would be there for her. She would be there for them. They would have so enjoyed each other.

For friendships are the best way to expand your horizons and keep from becoming isolated. How about you? You, too, have a vast assortment of acquaintances. In fact, they are likely too numerous to mention. Instead, write down a few organizations and groups where you find your acquaintances; church, business or former business, and such:

_____

_____

_____

_____

From that vast array, are there ten people (not necessarily couples themselves) whom you could call friend? Name some:

_____

_____

_____

_____

Where might you look should you wish to develop other

friendships than these? These should be places and organizations other than those mentioned above:

_____

_____

_____

_____

_____

Do you feel you are one of those people who needs more
friends than does your spouse? If so, where would you go to
meet people that your spouse probably would not?

_____

_____

Do you feel your spouse is more open to, and more needful
of, a wide variety of friends than you are? If so, what are some
of the ways you could encourage your spouse to get out and
associate with others?

_____

_____

_____

How might you encourage him/her to spend time with
these friends?

_____

_____

Cultivating friendships is quite another thing than meeting
them. What would be some ways in which you can make time
to be with your friends?

_____

_____

_____

The best and most lasting friend, however, has been and
always will be the person you married. In what ways specifically (that is, special to your life-style and you personally),
might you renew and enhance your friendship with your
spouse?

_____

_____

_____

Seeing with New Eyes

People in the Fifth Passage have been given a special gift. We call it the transcendent perspective. We've alluded obliquely to that gift in this chapter. Let us look at it more directly.

Chapter 6

A Transcendent Perspective

N asal cannula. Plural, *cannulae*. Both of these terms are much more official and scientific sounding than *little plastic tubes down your nose*. The Latin name can add much gloss to an otherwise unpleasant item. Carl Warden wagged his head and shifted in his easy chair beside Bess's bed. His brain sure came up with some stupid, silly stuff when it wandered.

Bess Warden mumbled something and raised one shoulder. Carl stood.

Gently, he helped her roll onto her side. Her spiderweb of nasal cannulae and IVs followed.

He patted her frail shoulder firmly. "Someone at the door, probably Butterfield. I'll be back in a shake, pet."

She mumbled a response as he left the room. His heels clicked hollow in the hallway. The house seemed so much bigger, so much emptier, these last few months. A lot of living happened in this house. A lot of living. And now, a dying.

It was nurse Janis Butterfield, all right, all six feet, two hundred pounds of her. Had Butterfield been a Texan, Santa Ana would never have made it through the door of the Alamo. She marched in without fanfare, a rather nervous young man at her heels.

"Hello, Carl. This is Bob McGruder, social services. He kept calling me up with questions about your case so I said, 'Bob, for crying out loud, come along with me this afternoon and ask Carl yourself.' So here he is. Did she sleep last night?"

"Pretty well. Pulse was a little shaky this morning, but she seems stronger now."

Butterfield nodded brusquely. "I'll give her injections and catch the record up. Keep this McGruder out of my hair, will you?" She charged off down the hall.

"Carl Warden, Mr. McGruder." Carl chuckled and extended his hand. "You look a little, ah, nonplussed. I take it you didn't meet Butterfield before today."

The man grinned suddenly and relaxed as he shook hands. "That obvious, huh? She comes on a bit strong, but I don't think I've ever met a nurse who knows her job better."

"You're right. Butterfield is the best there is. Bess and I are blessed by her. Come sit down. What do you want to know?" Carl led the way out to the patio. A moist breeze tempered the bright Indian Summer sun. It was a beautiful afternoon, a perfect afternoon. Bess's last autumn. Carl settled into a deck chair.

The social worker perched on a wrought iron chair at the patio table and popped open his briefcase. "Ms. Butterfield says you and Elizabeth have been married forty-nine years. Elizabeth is—let's see; here it is—Elizabeth is sixty-seven and you're sixty-eight. Her cancer was diagnosed just a few months ago, is that right?"

"Quite a jolt. She was feeling fine, and then one day she started feeling poorly and bam. We weren't expecting something like this. Guess we should have been, but we weren't."

"Only marriage for both of you, I assume."

Carl smiled. "High school sweethearts. Bess is the only girl I ever really fell for. Married late in '42 when I was on furlough, just before I shipped out to North Africa."

"Three children."

"Four. Our Becky died when she was two."

"Of . . . ?"

"Polio."

Mr. McGruder stopped and looked at Carl a minute. He spoke softly, thoughtfully. "How times change. I've never seen a case of polio. The Salk and Sabin vaccines came into use just before I was born. You've seen a lot of life, Mr. Warden, haven't you. Advances. More than a few reverses, too, I'll wager. A lot of pain."

Carl pursed his lips and thought about that a moment. "Yeah, I suppose you could say that. You could say Notre Dame cathedral is just another church too. Pain is part of it. I'm facing a lot of pain, losing Bess, and she has a lot of it right now. But it's not that. It's so much more than that. Limiting the measure of a lifetime to pain and joy is like asking a concert pianist to play Tchaikovsky's First with two fingers. It's—" Carl waved his hand helplessly. "I wish I could convey how very much it all is."

"No regrets? No reservations?"

"I wouldn't trade it for anything."

Transcendent Love

Were you to ask Carl Warden at twenty-five if he loved his Bess, he'd shout "Yes!" exuberantly. Ask him at thirty and he'd say, "Yeah, of course." At forty, the answer might be, "Deeply." Now, at the close of a life well lived, he might reply, "More than the day we married." And he would be speaking the truth, to the infinite power.

When the person who has made peace with life, with its warts and all, bumps into mortality and loss, those seemingly negative realities become fitting and appropriate conclusions to a life well lived. At the very least, they become something tolerable and tolerated. "Well lived" here does not mean brilliantly successful in every facet of life, but a life that is accepted as it is.

Transcendent love is a profound and peaceful perspective to-

ward your partner and toward life. Are your passages, particularly the Fifth, going smoothly, or have they been pockmarked with setbacks and tragedy? Transcendent love does not depend upon smoothness. It's not a tidy ribbon tied on the Fifth Passage package. It means, rather, that there has been a quantum shift in perspective. It is not that you somehow become oblivious to pain, that you suddenly can say an easy good-bye to all you cherish, but that you can rise above it.

"Let's say I'm trying to describe how ice cream tastes," Dr. Hemfelt explains. "I can lecture you for hours, and you still won't *really* know what ice cream is like. Similarly, I can hear about the peace of this Transcendent Love in my youth, but I cannot possibly know what it tastes like until I have the maturity, the wisdom, the life experience to get it from my head into my heart.

"It is not a cheap or shallow answer to the inevitable pain of loss. It is a profound dynamic. The older person can tell me what he sees from the top of the mountain, but it will all be abstract until I get there myself. Among the earliest Christian thinkers, there existed a long-standing tradition that as one moves closer to death, life becomes a more grace-filled experience."

Two major components make Transcendent Love what it is. The first is a paradox: The more I am able to let go of things, then ironically, the more I can truly value and cherish them. "Things" are human relationships, the bank account, physical health, material things—whatever I hold dear. Many persons facing advancing age feel that the key to transcendence seems to be acting on one or the other. Either I hang on with a possessive death grip (literally), or I have to devalue the things I care about, through estrangement, bitterness, anger. Either/or won't do it. Actually, the magic of this transcendent perspective lies in discovering the paradox.

Release things. By that we mean realize how transient things are, and that they cannot really be yours. As an example, consider an average couple in the Fifth Passage, their children grown now. Only if they say good-bye to their children's childhood, acknowledging the fact that they are now peers outside of parental control and possession, will that couple really appreciate, enjoy, and cherish their relationship with their children. Instead of spoiling or ending the relationship, releasing the kids allows parents freedom to pursue an easier, broader friendship not possible in any previous passages.

Can you think of friends or relatives who reversed this paradox, thus falling away from the transcendent perspective? Frequently we see an aging parent try to be more domineering and controlling (either through direct control or guilt-generating weakness). "If I can force you to love me, and if I cling tightly," the feeling goes, "I'll never have to face saying good-bye to you."

John Bradshaw, author of *Bradshaw on the Family* and *Homecoming* (Deerfield Beach, FL: Health Communications, 1988), reminds his listeners that you will leave or lose everyone and everything that you know in this human life. Such an ordinary truth—and yet, how extraordinary it is.

To the person who masters a Transcendent Love toward the spouse and toward life itself, the negative nature of that truth falls away, revealing dazzling hellos and doors of opportunity.

The other major component of Transcendent Love is the discovery of the relative disposition of things. Often people report that a brush with death changes the way they see things. What's important? Not important? What do I value? What counts and what doesn't?

This is why a portion of the population that experiences and most cherishes this Transcendent Perspective are those with terminal illnesses, those who have had near-death experiences, or those who've recovered from serious illness, a cancer patient for example.

A friend of ours met just such a person at a recent book

signing. She asked a specific author for one of his books on cancer. "I want it for my friend. He's only forty-four and has just been diagnosed with liver cancer." Tears came to our friend's eyes as she went on to relate the tragic story. The author was sympathetic but said the book was, unfortunately, out of print.

At the next table, however, another author overheard their conversation and came over. It seems this person was in remission from cancer. She spoke caringly and lovingly to our friend. It was a very moving experience for both of them.

When our friend asked why she had come over to talk with her, the woman replied, "My illness showed me never to pass up any chance for meaningful conversation with another human being. I saw you were hurting and I came over to talk to you. It would be the same if you were a stranger on the street. Human relationships are so much more important to me now."

So, as we become familiar with death, our lives change. The relative disposition of things around us changes. Nothing brings this as sharply into focus as a brush with death. Likewise, the aging process, by its very nature, forges that new perspective in the person who is willing to accept it.

Practical Ways in Which It Works for You

Shifting perspectives offer all sorts of new and exciting horizons.

May and Gary, Cody's grandparents (You remember Cody. Who could forget that imp?), received a serious jolt, literally and figuratively, when their van was broadsided by a pickup truck on I-20 east of town. May spent two days in intensive care and eight months learning how to walk well again. Gary fared better, with only some ribs broken, but he could not shake the memory of the vigil by May's bedside all those days in the hospital. Cody was eighty miles away from the accident, but it changes his life forever too.

For, as they sat in the hospital, and during the weeks afterward, May and Gary talked a lot about Cody. They could not baby-sit him during her convalescence; Cody plus physical therapy would have been one entanglement too many; but they could plan his life, at least so far as it touched upon them.

When May was well enough, they started taking Cody again, on a scheduled basis like before. They took him to fast food restaurants (his favorites) and fancy places (their preference). He learned not to throw peas at strangers. He even learned to fold his napkin. They took him to the amusement park. They took rides in the country and walks at the zoo. They housebroke Cody by dint of hard work and a whole lot of love.

Discipline accomplished it, just as they had housebroken their own children thirty years before. But this time the job turned out to be a whole lot easier, because now they had plenty of leisure time in which to build a happy relationship with Cody. Discipline without relationship will not work. Relationships first. May and Gary learned that about relationships with friends, and it worked with Cody too.

They felt freer and became much easier about parenting Cody on a part-time basis. They had more time than Cody's parents, and more patience. It wasn't just that retirement had given them extra hours. Their point of view toward life had shifted. In the course of eternity, what difference did it make if Cody didn't drink all his grape juice? So what if some of it landed on the rug? Cody was more important than a million rugs. And that message came through to him. His grandparents loved *him*.

Little Cody basked not in doting or adoration, not in rules and forced behavior, but in unconditional love. May and Gary could not have offered unconditional love ten years ago, or even five. It had always been "If you do this, we will . . ." Now it was, "We love you. Let's do this."

In a closing scene in Thornton Wilder's stage classic *Our Town*, the deceased Emily wants to witness one day in her life, something Wilder's dead were permitted to do. She watches a birthday from her past and gapes, stunned at how people attend so earnestly to trivia, allowing small irritations and distractions to spoil the moment. "Doesn't anyone really live life while they have it?" she cries. Her perspective had shifted, you see. From a viewpoint beyond death she realized how valuable each day is. So does the person in Transcendent Love.

The second task of the Fifth Passage of marriage is to achieve a transcendent perspective.

The Second Task: Achieve a Transcendent Perspective

Carl Warden watched Bob McGruder and Nurse Butterfield ride away in Butterfield's snazzy little sports car. He smiled. She refused to drive the official county car with the emblem on the door; "I look too much like a bureaucrat in those things," she grumped. He went back inside.

Was Bess awake? He walked quietly back to the bedroom. She was.

He rubbed her frail, bony little shoulder. "Chicken for supper?"

"Sounds fine," she murmured.

Why did he ask her when, until he ran down to the store, all they had in the fridge was a chicken? Because he didn't want her to lose her sense of being part of the partnership. Was that it? He thought a moment. That was it. They had always run decisions past each other, usually as a courtesy. No reason to change now.

With a heavy sigh he wandered out to the kitchen to see what else was in the fridge.

Carl was facing a severe good-bye. He knew that. So will you—either you or your spouse, no matter what passage your marriage is in.

We mentioned that Transcendent Love is a perspective toward life. Transcendent Love is not a process people can go through; it's a true shift in perspective. How does one make the shift?

Consider each of two contrasting statements. The first statement can be attributed to a young or immature outlook, the second to Transcendent Love. Where is the link; what was the shift? Apply the two statements to your own thinking and your own circumstance. Which of these statements matches your own perspective?

Suffering is meaningless vs. suffering creates new places in the human heart and soul. "Suffering builds character," the father in the Calvin and Hobbes cartoon remonstrates. "I don't want any more character," Calvin pouts.

When suffering looms, a part of us repeats Calvin's protest. Who needs this? But a greater part of us can know that when inevitable suffering comes, it can serve a constructive purpose if we allow it to. Remember the paradox upon which Transcendent Love depends? Only as I am willing to release it can I enjoy and appreciate it. By bringing to sharper focus the finite limitations of human life, suffering helps the sufferer see life clearly. By seeing it clearly, and in a way touching it tangibly, the sufferer can more easily release that life. It's hard enough to work in abstracts; fuzzy abstracts are hardest of all to grasp. The end result: the sufferer better enjoys that life which he or she has.

Joni Eareckson Tada, while never welcoming quadriplegia, has dedicated her life and ministry to helping others understand the extraordinary blessings that come out of extreme suffering such as hers. Suffering itself helped her make the shift to her transcendent perspective earlier than most. Suffering, then, need not be a roadblock or a barrier, but a facilitator—a point of leverage to push you over into that rewarding and comforting perspective of Transcendent Love.

Aging equals loneliness vs. aging equals greater intimacy. From the transcendent perspective, you've been working on getting to know your spouse better through four passages of marriage encompassing many years. Intimacy has been growing. Besides, you now know yourself much better than you did even a few years ago.

An elderly patient of Dr. Hemfelt's offered a wonderful insight. When Robert kidded her, "I see you've put most of your denial down," she replied, "After you've been through all I've been through, you learn not to lie, especially to yourself."

With years of living behind you, you probably have a better capacity to cherish the relationships in your life. As an opposite of loneliness, you find relationships more enriching.

A recent survey asked people in nursing homes what physical possession they valued most. First on the list everywhere was "pictures of relatives." Rob them of their TV and their jewelry, but don't dare touch the photos by their bed.

As couples in the Fifth Passage sift through memories, using the measure of relative disposition, they come to cherish relationships more than younger people do. "This is what is important; that is not." Dr. Paul Warren, behavioral pediatrician of the Minirth-Meier Clinic in Dallas, teaches even very young children in his counsel that relationships are everything. That comes to bear here.

Physical loss is absolute loss vs. physical loss is spiritual emancipation. In one of his "Focus on the Family" radio programs, Dr. James Dobson commented of material possessions, "Everything I own owns me." There is nothing wrong with having physical possessions, but they all come with a price tag. To the extent we take them on, they drain us, deplete us. They require emotional and spiritual maintenance.

As people move through this final passage, they either gradually begin to let go of the physical or cling to it inordinately. As the significance of the physical (health, possessions, all things physical) wanes, the persons begin to pump more psychic energy into non-material things, including the hereafter and love itself. Persons making a desperate effort to hang onto the physical are drained by it. This depletes the emotional and spiritual energy needed to shift up into the transcendent perspective.

You can compare this phenomenon roughly with the old Star Trek concept of warp drive—speeds faster than the speed of light. In some episodes, a crisis would deplete the starship's power, preventing it from making the leap to warp speed, condemning it to slog along at a snail's pace.

People make the shift into transcendence, in part, by gradually surrendering ownership of the material world around them. Instead of feeling like a loss, this surrender becomes liberating. Many couples who planned wisely will start bequeathing some of their money before death. There are often tax advantages, true. But the deeper meaning is to divest oneself of the material, lightening the load.

Time is rushing, slipping away vs. time, being eternal, can slow down. Find a conventional watch or clock face with a sweep second hand. Stare at it for a few minutes. The second hand will visibly slow down. In theory, if astronauts orbit in a particular direction long enough and fast enough, they will return to earth younger than when they left. Time is an amazing flexible phenomenon.

To four-year-old Rachel, the week prior to her birthday is a year long. An afternoon in the park, with plenty of fun and running around, seems like days. Time elongates for children and a year is a long, long time. Not so for the person in midlife. The thirty-nine-year-old celebrates a birthday and the next day must celebrate the fortieth. A lot of studio greeting cards and jokes tease about how time speeds up as we get older. But time does an about-face in the Fifth Passage, for those people who can accept life. Instead of flying rapidly, accelerating up to the time of death, time pauses, to let those people smell the flowers.

An acquaintance, Tony, who is well over sixty-five, phrased it this way: "My wife and I do a lot of kayaking. We've ridden some rough stuff—class three water. The cascades spill you this way and that, slam you around, send you shooting down the rapids. Heavy water like that, though, has still spots. You swing your craft around and sneak behind a boulder, or in a little cove to the side called an eddy, and the water can rush by all it wants. You're on calm water. We call it eddying out. Then you eddy back in and it's down the chute you go again."

People with a transcendent perspective find themselves eddying out of the rush of time now and then. They can savor moments of time; literally, time stands still. "A precious moment when I stepped out of the stream of time," Tony said, "was when I kissed my new little great grandson on the head. There he was, eight weeks old, and—" Tony's voice catches.

A woman at a bedside vigil with her dying mate reported that during those days, there were many moments when time seemed to stand still.

Another way this phenomenon shows itself is that older people have the capacity to slow down. The reduced pace may be physically necessary to some degree. But also, it reflects the shift of perspective inside. The person no longer has to go faster and faster. If it takes fifteen minutes to walk out to the mailbox, that's all right. The youngster might call it wasting time. The person with a new perspective will not.

"It's like the stream ripping down through the canyon, and then dumping out into a lake or reservoir," Tony relates. "Suddenly it's serene. You go only as fast as you want to. That's what it feels like to me."

What Tony was really doing had far more profound significance than simply appreciating time. He was preparing to move into eternal time. Making peace here with the temporal boundaries, he was starting to leave behind his temporal perspective and shift into the eternal, non-time perspective.

Christian theologians phrase it as, "It's important to try to learn how to live in the eternal now." Long before death, we can discover small ways to step out of the stream of time, providing glimpses and foretastes of what eternity is like. We often do this when we make time to watch the peaceful motion of the rippling waters of a beautiful lake, or stroll a lush, green golf course as the sun is setting. We do it in the most significant way when we join in worship of God with others or hold hands together in a circle of prayer. We find profound peace.

Beginning the Journey

We cannot overemphasize the role good preparation plays in dealing with death—your loved ones' and yours.

"That sounds so morbid!" you protest.

"Not at all," we reply. When you expect a baby's arrival you have the diapers, the necessary furniture, the baby clothes ready and waiting. When you go into the hospital for surgery, you make arrangements in advance. You don't troop off on vacation without packing a suitcase. Preparation smooths the way when any unusual event looms on the horizon.

Mary Alice Minirth's father prepared for his wife financially. He set up funds and accounts for her and put their financial records in order. Mentally and emotionally, they prepared themselves as best they could by talking about what the future held, reminiscing about the past, grieving the approaching end, rejoicing in the safety which their risen Lord promises.

During the last year before his death, Mary Alice's mother received important support from her church. Prayer support was primary. Prayer truly does effect amazing things. If you can do nothing else for friends or loved ones facing loss, pray for them. The pastor and congregation of her parents' church made certain their practical needs were met. In your church, do you have elderly members with everyday needs you can meet?

"At the funeral, that support never faltered," says Mary Alice. "Pastor said to Mom, 'Now, sister Francis, you know that half of you is gone.' He counseled her with facts. 'You have to realize this and this.' He never whitewashed bad points. But he reminded her 'God will sustain.'"

Mary Alice's mother didn't leave the Richardson area right away. She tied up loose ends, eventually left, then returned when Mary Alice's latest baby arrived. She and six other widows in her church support each other. They have lunch together; they attend a seniors' club. Mary Alice calls her, asking about activities, and encouraging them. The daughter is helping the mother to avoid shutting off.

Both of them know that to shut off is dangerous. "Circumstances happen," Mary Alice concludes. "They're not your choice. But your response to them is your choice."

Because Carl and Bess Warden felt in the pink of health, they did not concern themselves with the legal, medical, and social aspects of sudden illness. Somehow, it almost seems like a twisted sort of wish-fulfillment to read up on death and illness. If you ignore it, it won't knock on your door.

It doesn't work that way, of course. Your head tells you so, although your heart still shies away from the subject. So put your head to work. Carl had to come from behind when Bess got sick. He did not know what options were available to him. Did she have to leave her home? Who would pay for what? Was their insurance adequate? What about Medicare? He did a lot of cramming in a hurry, and even then he wasn't sure that the perfect solution didn't lie out there somewhere, undetected.

A friend of ours confides, "This sounds morbid, but I have a list of things to do in the first three days if my husband dies suddenly. I keep it in the lockbox in the closet. If something should happen to him, I'll get it out and just go down the list: Whom to notify first, whom to write letters to, whom to call about arrangements . . . I figure I'll be in no mental condition to have to work all that out when it happens."

She's being wise, not morbid. Her husband should be doing exactly the same thing.

Preparation—learning in advance what agencies and services are available, what insurance payment plans will and will not cover, what each spouse must do and when—opens several bright doors. One of them is peace of mind. You have the future nailed down as well as you can. You don't have to fret about it and dread it so much, should the time arise. You have just eliminated a whole category of worries. Also, preparation provides you and your children with a solid plan of action, yet not something set in cement. If circumstances alter, the plan can be altered; but you have something to start with.

Preparation for eventual separation serves another important purpose, it brings fears and sad thoughts into clear focus. Only when you acknowledge them can you deal with them. That's right. You want to grieve your spouse's mortality (and your own) just as you grieved the other imperfections of life.

Good-bye . . .

Carl Warden wandered down the street to the park, and the quiet duck pond. His house was bustling just now with friends, neighbors, kids, and grandkids. He wanted to get away a few minutes. Then he'd jump back in, making the final arrangements.

They had talked about this day, Bess and he. They speculated what it would be like. They joked about it. Joking helps relieve the pain of reality. On one occasion, Bess explained what she wanted in the way of final rites. On another, Carl talked about what he wanted. Neither of them bound the other to their wishes with idle promises. Each knew what the other wanted; that was enough. They discussed which children would receive what among their personal possessions. Bess wanted Annie to have the mantel clock her own great-grandfather brought from the old country. Annie appreciated that kind of thing. Carl would see to it.

Bess had also asked Carl to sing at her funeral. He decided he would not do that. His voice no longer had the quality it used to. He'd let his buddy Al do the singing; Al was still a hearty baritone. Besides, his voice would probably break. His heart had already.

Jamie would fly in this afternoon; Rob was probably already on his way to the airport to pick him up. Not everyone was as lucky as Carl, who would have all his family around him at the funeral. In fact, Carl was twice-times lucky. Between him and all his kids and grandkids there were no rifts, no factions, no guarded hostility.

That wasn't true for Al and his son. Maybe one of these days Carl would talk to Al about how important relationships had become to him. He knew for a fact how much happier Al would be were that rift repaired.

He reached the pond shore. The resident ducks, goofy-looking mallard-and-something mixed breeds, came gabbling over to him. Carl had forgotten the stale bread. No matter. These fat, saucy ducks certainly weren't depending on Carl for their next meal. The water slapped and sloshed at his feet, churning, and yet, peaceful.

Bess.

Chapter 7

Completing the Passage Without a Partner

Q uincy was dead; you could tell it by looking at him. Briskly, a paramedic who couldn't be more than a few years out of high school slapped three big round pads on Quincy's chest and connected him up to a portable heart monitor.

Sally watched, so engulfed by the whole thing she felt numb. Four times that week, and it was only Thursday night, she had taken Quincy to various doctors, including one trip to the emergency room. The doctors lived in two different cities and the hospital was thirty-seven miles away. Until this moment, she had prepared all his meals according to a special diet and made sure he got all his medicines. Sally was tired. But when you've been married to a man for over fifty years, you do that.

The paramedic's assistant, a cute little girl with honey-gold hair, explained, "That's a defibrillator. If his heart has gone into ventricular fibrillation, we can restore the beat."

Sally shook her head. "If you bring him back, he'll be very angry."

Across the state another death was happening, another widow being created. Leora's husband Walt, a cancer victim, passed away in the hospital, connected to a maze of tubes. The passing was unremarkable, if any death can be called so, in that he died quietly in his sleep.

The same funeral home attended to both Walt and Quincy. There any similarity ended.

SALLY: Sally, now matriarch of her family by default, let her three sons and two daughters wait upon her, handle her immediate affairs, and, in consultation with her, take care of final arrangements. As much as she needed some help, she knew, they needed something positive and important to do.

LEORA: Leora, who had assumed the matriarchy when Walt was first diagnosed with cancer, had no choice but to let her children wait upon her. She did not drive, did not handle the finances, did not arrange any funeral particulars in advance. Walt always took care of that sort of thing. And so she told the kids what she wanted done, and what arrangements she wanted made, and where she wanted to go. From her kids' perspective, not a whole lot had changed.

SALLY: In the first weeks after the funeral, Sally was sorely tempted to sell off the family farm here and move into town. She hated the long drive whenever she wanted to go somewhere and do something. And the memories of Quincy haunted her so. Her children asked her not to, for her own sake, and so she did not.

The kids were right. The bad memories of Quincy faded and the good ones clung to the old house. She could putter in her garden and lose herself in her library of old books. She reread some favorite novels, deadheaded the roses and geraniums, piddled around, and let time do its work on her soul.

LEORA: Because Leora could not drive, she could not keep the house she and Walt had lived in for thirty-five years. It was too far from the grocery store, the doctor's, the bank, the drugstore. Besides, she was getting too rickety to climb the stairs. She insisted that her children could simply come by once or twice each day, taking turns, and meet whatever needs she had at the moment. Her children resisted the idea. She insisted. She won, for awhile, basically because she was so good at laying guilt trips on the kids.

Her eldest son eventually moved her bodily out of the family home. He arranged an auction to dispose of the household goods he and his sisters did not want, and placed the money in an account earmarked for Mom's care. Leora was furious, but what could she do? They moved her into the son's home, but when he got the ultimatum from his wife, "It's your mother or me, but we're not both going to live under this roof," he moved Leora into an assisted living facility.

SALLY: Four months after Quincy's death, Sally's grandson announced his wedding. In Michigan. Sally had never flown, had never been more than three hundred miles from the farm. She made arrangements to attend, assisted by a travel agent her daughter recommended, and spent an afternoon purchasing the first luggage she had ever owned.

"My life," she declared to a friend, "is in turmoil. But it's a happy turmoil." Ripped by dread and delicious anticipation, she embarked on the adventure of a lifetime. Within the next year, she would also travel to Anchorage for another grandson's graduation, attend a reunion of Quincy's family in Ann Arbor, and take a Caribbean cruise with friends from church. Her social security couldn't handle quite all the travel expenses, so her children cheerfully and enthusiastically helped out. It embarrassed her. She hated accepting money from them. But it seemed to delight them so.

LEORA: Leora ended up in four different facilities in the year after Walt died, not counting her son's home. No facility met her exacting needs and preferences. None was friendly, none served her adequately. She lost confidence in her son and attached herself instead to the elder of the three daughters. Nancy knew how Leora felt. Nancy understood her. Nancy wouldn't treat her shabbily the way the other children did. Besides, Nancy was divorced, so there would not be the friction that in-law relationships always generate.

Then Nancy became involved with an absolutely horrible man, and moved to Connecticut. Leora had to reassess her opinion of Janet, the middle daughter. Janet was married. Janet wouldn't abandon her own mother the way Nancy did. Leora never forgave Nancy for moving two thousand miles away and getting married.

SALLY: The day came when Sally couldn't drive safely anymore. It took her minutes and minutes to negotiate the stairs in the farmhouse because her hips were starting to go. She accepted the inevitable and, with her kids' help, found a nice little ground-floor apartment within five blocks of a mall. She transferred her accounts to the bank there. Now she could walk to just about every place she had to be. Her travel days were about done, but my, didn't she have a good time while she was able!

In the soft glow of her many memories, Sally was able to come to a transcendent love of her husband even beyond death. They had stayed the course. They had finished the race. The prize was theirs.

And she still missed dear, testy old Quincy terribly.

LEORA: The light of Leora's life was her grandchildren. In retrospect, Leora's kids agreed that a major reason she loved the grandkids so was because they were not responsible for her powerlessness. In her eyes, she held her children accountable for the shuffling about she suffered, for the inability to live life as she wanted.

But, she told her children, it was really all Walt's fault. He went on and left her behind. He was the one who did all this to her. She still missed him terribly, but she could never ever forgive him.

Guidelines

We dwelt at some length on the stories of Sally and Leora because the two women so vividly illustrate the good and the bad of going on without a spouse. Their example also illustrates some guidelines we've found to work at this difficult time of separation. The fact that both are women is of little importance. Men face the same challenges and heartaches women do. They either meet them or are defeated by them in the same ways as women. The situation of going on alone is not gender specific.

Accept Trusted Counsel

Sally instinctively knew that her children had needs as pressing as hers. Their father had just passed away. They needed to be a part of the closure of his life, not just lackeys under the direction of others. Had her children not been there, Sally could have handled everything herself. But they were, and she dealt them in. Sharing this experience immensely profited both Sally and her kids. More important, she realized she did not have all the answers, particularly at this tragic time, and accepted their advice.

Leora had to pull all the strings. She could not bring herself to trust the help and decisions of her adult children. When they did make decisions on her behalf, she either undermined them or found fault with them.

Perhaps Leora had a right to find fault. Perhaps her children's decisions were selfish, immature, or thoughtless. Her track record of residences she found unacceptable suggests, though, that she gave none of her children's decisions a chance.

Leora would have done much better to make decisions in concert with her children as Sally did, bending here, standing firm there, working out a good course of action.

Accept that the Loss Is Irreplaceable

Leora's gravest mistake was to replace her spouse with her kids. In essence, she shifted her dependence directly from Walt to her son and daughters. In her eyes they had no right to move away, as did Nancy, or refuse to tie themselves to her daily service.

"Many times in counseling," claims Brian Newman, "I sit with a person whose only real problem is guilt for having a life independent of his or her aging parents. Guilt for being your own person? Guilt for living your life? No. There should be no such thing. In every person I've counseled, their guilt is false. In fact, they really do take good care of their parents. Every person. And in almost every case, the parents are laying the guilt trip." Brian adds, "I would suspect, though, that the people who actually do neglect their parents to the parents' detriment don't have guilt problems. They aren't coming to see me for that reason."

One of the greatest gifts you can give your children, a gift Sally gave hers, is surcease from guilt.

Accept Your New Identity

Leora had no identity apart from "wife" or "mother." She was never just Leora. Sally, too, started her widowhood as wife and mother. But once the first numbing crush of grief subsided, she began to build an identity that was hers alone, "Sally the widow." She forced herself, at times against her own will, into situations that made her grow. In particular, travel demanded that she function as an individual, a woman on her own.

The ability to travel didn't last. The individuality did.

Leora, though, could not safely travel the way Sally did. It probably would have been unwise for Leora to take off and go places, though had she been forced into it she would have managed well. Leora, however, could have built her identity and independence in other ways. Among them:

- Joining a club her kids were not involved with
- Becoming more active in her church
- Undertaking community service that interested her
- Engaging in at-home correspondence for any of numerous organizations that would welcome her help—missions, conservation groups, political organizations, special-interest clubs and groups
- Help handle annual fund-raising sales for various service clubs or groups, such as Girl Scout cookies, white canes, flags, Red Cross drives and blood drives

Leora would have been horrified, no doubt, were she to hear of Sally's adventures. Look at Sally, abandoning her children when they needed her most! Of course, that was not so. Sally considered her children as equal adults equally involved in getting through life. Sally did not cling to her children in a death grip.

Leora did.

To Think About

Here's an exercise we recommend for couples, macabre as it may sound: Assume your spouse suddenly and unexpectedly passed away.

1. What will you do first?

_____

_____

_____

2. Whom will you notify by phone?

_____

_____

_____

3. What mailing list will you mail notices or notes to?

_____

_____

_____

4. What funeral/interment arrangements must you make?

_____

_____

_____

5. Prepare to be aware of the grieving process inside you. You know yourself well by now. What signs and indications of

each of these steps have you learned to recognize within yourself?

a. "Shock and denial evidences itself in me with:

_____

_____

_____ . "

b. "In me, anger generated by death and other losses usually
surfaces in these ways:

_____

_____

_____ . "

Toward whom?

_____

c. "Depression reveals itself in these behaviors of mine:

_____

_____

_____ . "

d. "I've caught myself bargaining before. Some instances:

_____

_____

_____ . "

e. "True sadness is an old friend of mine. I show these behaviors:

_____

_____

_____ . "

For how long, usually?

_____

6. This time of loss is rife with the need to forgive and be
forgiven. You have these acts of forgiveness to bestow and
request:

_____ Your spouse, for leaving you

_____ Your spouse, for not leaving behind a tidy estate all
arranged, with nothing you have to do.

_____ Your children, for thoughtlessness, especially at this time
_____ God
_____ Others:

_____

_____

Of whom should you ask forgiveness?

_____

_____

_____

7. With whom among your friends would you like most to associate during the first six months following the loss?

_____

_____

_____

8. After the initial mourning, to whom would you feel most compelled to reach out as a comforter and benefactor?

_____

_____

_____

Reaching out to others is a gracious gift, and older people seem to possess it with special flair. It is a part of what we might call living on in style.

Living on in Style

"My grandmother." Mary Alice Minirth smiles at the thought. "She spent her last years in a nursing home, and she was in her nineties. She loved my grandfather and was very sad about being left behind. She kept asking, 'I'm blind and deaf. Why doesn't God take me?'

"She sang gospel songs in her room. God's gift to her to the very end was a clear, sweet voice. I am not trying to second-guess God, but possibly one of the reasons was to allow her to be a blessing. And she was a blessing to so many people, more than she ever realized."

Despite her loneliness, the lady lived on with style.

"And then there was my grandfather," a friend named Erica recalls. "He still drove the L.A. freeways when he was ninety. His kids—sixty-year-old kids!—took his license away from him when he backed out of his drive and hit his mailbox. Powdered it. But up to his death four years later, he still collected and shelled walnuts for charity. He ran his own life and wanted to run everyone else's too. Crusty old gent! We loved him.

"I think he knew when the end was coming. He refused to enter a nursing home. He wanted all his grandchildren and great grandchildren to come visit at Christmas. This was in '91. Some of us came from a thousand miles away, literally, and a couple of the grandchildren went into debt to make the trip. Every single one was there. He died on January 15."

Erica sat thoughtfully a few moments. "You know, we all did it as a favor to Grandpa. But actually, we were the ones who benefited most. It's the only time we've all been in the same place at the same time. It's the first time, I think, that many of us realized how important our extended family is. We're going to get together every couple of years now thanks to him showing the way."

Erica's grandfather lived on with style.

The Final Task

No matter how long you remain together as a couple, no matter how long one of you survives the other, building your own identity again and living in style is the next-to-the-last real task in life. The final task, the final achievement, is also the most satisfying. If you and your spouse can help each other in it, it will be all the more satisfying. But it is the step one must ultimately take alone.

Chapter 8

Can You Accept Your One and Only God-Given Life?

I n the classic Disney film *Old Yeller*, the lead character, a charming scalawag of a dog, captures the hearts of a pioneer family whose father/husband must leave for a time. The dog acts heroically and in the process contracts rabies. The half-grown son destroys his beloved companion to spare it the agony of slow suffering and a certain, horrible death.

The father returns, and his words of wisdom to ease his son's heartache can be applied far beyond the circumstances in that motion picture. They also frame a philosophy that describes this Fifth Passage to a tee. With that philosophy, the whole of your history and experience work together to strengthen what can be the best years of your life.

Father and son converse beneath a tree on a hill. The father: "Thing to do now is try and forget it—go on being a man."

"How, Pa? How ya gonna forget something like that?"

"I guess I don't quite mean that. It's not a thing you can forget. Maybe not even a thing you want to forget. What I'm trying to say is, life's like that sometimes."

"Like what?"

"Well, now and then for no good reason a man can figure out, life will just haul off and knock him flat, slam him ag'in the ground so hard it seems like all his insides is busted. It's not all like that. A lot of it is mighty fine. You can't afford to waste the good part frettin' about the bad. That makes it all bad. You understand what I'm trying to get at?"

"Yes sir. It's just that—"

"Sure, I know. Saying it's one thing; feeling it's another. But I'll tell you a trick that's sometimes a big help. Start looking around for something good to take the place of the bad. As a general rule, you can find it."

Frettin' about the Losses

Is the person who loves transcendently freed of the need to grieve? Not at all. There still remain the anger, fear and depression, bargaining, sadness, and acceptance. But the acceptance, the fruit of grief, extends to satisfying new dimensions.

The third task of this Fifth Passage is to come to terms with your own death. We phrase the task this way: "My acceptance of my own death requires that I have accepted my one and only God-given life." If you, like Carl Warden, lose a spouse early in the Fifth Passage, your spouse's death will force you to accept your own mortality early in the passage. The sooner you make peace with your own mortality, the more joyous this passage will be.

The Third Task: To Accept My One and Only
God-Given Life

The extent to which I have trouble accepting my own death may reflect a major way in which I have not accepted some past or present aspect of living. Trouble includes exaggerated fear, depression, anger, and bitterness. Moreover, if I have many exaggerated fears, anger, or denial about my inevitable losses and good-byes, that tells me that I have failed as yet to make peace with (that is, accepted) some aspect of my living.

Getting Stuck

A woman, Grace, in our counsel, took her mother into her home in 1968, when her father died. Until last year she cared for her mother, providing everything for the woman. (Grace is also widowed.)

Then Momma broke a hip and Grace could not physically take care of her. Necessity forced Grace to place Momma in a nursing home. The first thing Momma said when Grace walked in the door to visit her was, "You betrayed me." A quarter century of constant care and effort meant nothing. In her mother's eyes, Grace had abandoned her. What went on here?

As we took Grace into counseling, we explored the probability (a very high probability) that Grace and her mother both had become mired in one of several possible swamps: either they had become stuck in a prior passage of marriage, or they had become stuck in some step of the grieving process.

Persons who are stuck in a previous passage cannot achieve the transcendent love of the Fifth. If they get bogged down in a stage of grieving, they cannot reach resolution. Resolution and acceptance are critical parts of transcendent love. Grace's Momma got stuck in the bargaining phase of grief and Grace was suffering the fallout just as much as Momma was. We find it very common for persons in the Fifth Passage to get stuck in the bargaining stage.

Perhaps instead of accepting that life is coming to an end, and possibly taking appropriate steps to distribute their estate, a couple starts hoarding money even more. How often do we hear of elderly persons, living alone in penury, who have stashed thousands of dollars in their mattress? The bargain there is, "If I can hoard enough financial security, somehow, I'll not have to face the final losses." It's not a conscious bargain. It certainly makes no intellectual sense. Often, bargaining is neither conscious nor intellectual.

Another couple may take up a fanatical preoccupation with physical health. "If I can only remain vigilant enough about my health, I won't die." (And the clincher: "It's worked so far, hasn't it?")

Had Grace's Dad not passed away, even if Momma had not spent twenty-some years under Grace's roof, Grace's mom would probably be stuck at the bargaining stage anyway. "If I can just cling closely enough to my daughter, her youth will carry me through. I won't lose everything." Grace's problems and her mother's arose out of their past. Grace's mother had never really wedded well to Dad; they never established a close emotional bond. Grace's Momma drew from Grace to meet her intimacy needs, particularly after Dad died. Grace, with scantly met emotional needs of her own, became a party to it. Their final years were simply a magnification of what had been going on for most of their lives.

Beware also the contingent life. The person living a contingent life is always waiting for life to start. "When I graduate from high school, I can really live. No, wait; make that after I graduate from college. Actually, when I get married is when life really starts. But I have to get the career going first, then I'll really enjoy life . . . When I retire I'll really be happy . . ."

The person living a contingent life never accepts, "This is my life now, and I will enjoy it now." Life is not a dress rehearsal.

When that person arrives at the Fifth Passage, deep, deep bitterness and anger boil up as the truth hits: "My life is coming to end and I haven't lived yet."

Persons overcome by that realization may go through a period of agnosticism, doubting the value of everything in life from God on down. "What happened to dear old George?" the neighbors ask. "He used to be so dependable. So regular. Now here he is consumed with bitterness. What kind of example is that for the younger folks?"

Dodging Death

"Can't be done," you say. "Spiritually, yes. Not physically."

We agree. But that's just your head speaking. A lot of people, unable to come to terms with losses, make strange pledges in their heart where their head has no say. Dodging death here includes not just physical death, but symbols of impending death such as deteriorating health, departed youth, loss of a driver's license—those things that serve as mileposts to the final day.

Seven common pitfalls, seven death dodgers, bar a person from reaching transcendent love. Which one a person picks depends on which way that person's family-of-origin shaped him or her. Even more, how that person negotiated the previous passages of marriage will determine whether the person gets hung up in one of these death dodgers. See if any of these death dodgers have ever occurred to you:

_____ *Hypochondria.* Hypochondriacs constantly imagine illnesses or inflate existing illness. The symptoms and the pain are absolutely real, but they are not caused by the agents normally associated with them. Stress and emotion generate them. We call this psychogenic illness. Gerontologists agree that they have to sift through a lot of psychogenic symptoms to find organic problems.

Hypochondria serves two purposes. It is a way to dodge death and mortality; "If I can be vigilant enough, I will outmaneuver death. Lethal problems cannot sneak up on me." Also, hypochondria is a way to indirectly grieve death. Long before death actually comes, the person has grieved, literally, hundreds of little deaths. Indefinable illnesses. It's the mind and body's way of staging a miniature death experience over and over, preparing for the big one. In a way, it works. The grieving process is served. But it's not a good way, for the pain is real, and fear and worry drain away happiness. There is no calm and peace for the hypochondriac. It is only an escalation of pain and fear as the end actually comes.

_____ *Bitterness and Cynicism.* Anyone in any passage of marriage can become bitter and cynical, but the persons dodging death raise it to an art form. These persons are headed in the opposite direction from transcendent love. Instead of serenity and acceptance, they promote friction and refusal. We believe the underlying, unspoken motivation here can be expressed, "If I cannot reach a perspective of transcendent love (because of failure to complete prior passages) I will move radically in the opposite direction." It's exceedingly common in the elderly.

Ebenezer Scrooge in Dickens's *A Christmas Carol* is the quintessential example. So is Silas Marner. If their perspective gets turned upside down—reversed by ghosts or by circumstance—they are quite capable of achieving acceptance and serenity.

Bitterness does two things. It channels off the anger and frustration about not being able to reach a transcendent perspective. Too, it becomes, in a way, almost a rationalization for avoiding the transcendent perspective. "If I can poke enough holes in tranquility, and become cynical enough about God and meaning and life, I don't have to mourn the pain of not having all that."

_____ *Health Obsession.* Twenty thousand units daily of vitamin C is the key to life, or perhaps two slices of whole wheat bread, or maybe blackstrap molasses. There is an immense and profitable (for the producers) body of literature available for and by people who buy into super-health for prolonging life. An offshoot of this is the practice of freezing a body until such time as a cure is found for its terminal illness or other problem, or until rejuvenation has been perfected.

_____ *Suicide.* This is the flip side of health obsession. Suicide includes slow or passive suicide. For example, an elderly person might stop eating. It happens often. "Why?" you ask. The person shrugs, at a loss for a valid reason. "No appetite. Nothing tastes good anymore." That person is moving away from transcendent love.

Instead of accepting the brevity and transience of life, enabling them to appreciate and cherish it, such persons say, deep inside, "Life is transient and fleeting and that is so frightening that the only way I can handle it is to shorten it deliberately. If I can't master it, I shall take the power of life and death into my own hands." The dread of uncertainty makes them want to seize the power to end it on their own terms. When the doctor tells the person to walk a mile a day, and the person doesn't; when the person consciously fails to take prescribed medicine—all are manifestations of this. The person who can accept the transitory nature of life, we've found, will be a better steward of life, living it sensibly and well.

_____ *Counterfeit Transcendence.*   All through life, Herb's faith had been, at best, lukewarm. He limited it to Sundays in a mainstream church and didn't think about it much the rest of the week—until he moved into the Fifth Passage. His parents died. His sister died. His wife became ill. His arthritis became so bad he had to give up golf. Suddenly Herb became pious. "Religious fanatic" was not too strong a label for him. "Religiously addicted" hit the nail on the head. He embraced a fringe church some would call a cult because it offered exaggerated promises of human perfection. If Herb just had enough faith, ordinary human pain would elude him.

_____ *Hate God, Fate, and/or Circumstances.*   Brett's father lost the family fortune during the Depression. Brett salvaged a snip of the family business and worked hard for nearly fifty years to keep it afloat. When Brett retired he sold the business, but not for much. Brett had never fully grieved what his father had lost, nor had the father. Brett did not grieve and celebrate the heroic struggle he himself had made. Now in Brett's Fifth Passage, what had started out as anger about the family business had mushroomed until it encompassed everything. Brett was angry and suspicious of all things. We call this low-grade paranoia.

If you yourself feel overwhelmed by the unfairness and pain of the past, look for losses you and your family accrued earlier that might not have been grieved and worked through. Those unresolved losses draw interest through time, growing and magnifying, so that by the Fifth Passage they burst forth in highly magnified form.

_____ *Those Time-Release Capsules.* The ones we spoke about in the first chapter. Hidden agendas or unfinished business handed down to you from your parents or from your parents' parents.

When Franklin Delano Roosevelt died, his wife grieved deeply, picked up the pieces, and went on to greatness in her own right. When Prince Albert died, Queen Victoria descended into a sorrow and depression from which she never recovered. A man in our counsel, married 45 years, left his wife. It took a while to uncover his deepest, darkest motivations. The man was terrified of death. He never made peace with it. His mother and father, his brothers and sisters all experienced extreme difficulty saying good-bye. He was running away from marriage, but what he really was running away from was ever having to face the future death of his spouse.

Even now in the Fifth Passage, forty years or so after your departure from your childhood home, those time-release capsules still influence you; often they are not activated until you reach the age at which your parents faced these issues. You may, in fact, be trying to dodge death in the way they did. How did your parents and grandparents come to terms with mortality? Think about your siblings' attitudes too; they are subject to the same cross-generational influences you are.

Have you made peace with your own mortality? You will wrestle (or are wrestling) with this yourself. Know that your family's attitudes shape your own. Take a moment now to look back.

When did my parents sit down with me to discuss illness and death?

_____ When my favorite pet died
_____ When my grandfather or grandmother died
_____ When my brother or sister died
_____ When my mom or dad died
_____ When a playmate died

What did they say to me at this time? (For instance, perhaps they said, "Grandpa has gone to a better place." Or, "He's gone to be with the Lord, and we will see him again some day.")

_____

_____

How old were my parents when my grandparents died? __
How did my parents treat it? (For instance, did Dad talk about the fun times he had with Grandpa fishing or playing ball? Or did he refuse to talk about him? Or did Mom cry every time someone mentioned Grandma for a couple of years?)

_____

_____

Has my parents' attitude toward death influenced my own attitude?   _____ yes   _____ no

One male patient inherited the attitude, "When a man stops working, he dies," from his father. Prior to the man's retirement he and his wife joked about that legacy. One year into his retirement that was no longer a joke. It had become a reality. The man was gorging himself with food, but he had stopped playing golf or walking or doing much of anything else.

His wife confronted him with that old family legacy and suggested counseling. In the next weeks the man realized he was, in fact, living out that legacy. He was startled by how powerful that time-release capsule had been; he had not planned to neglect himself in those first nine months.

Could you be living out an old family legacy? Could your attitude toward death reflect your parents?
If so, how?

_____

_____

Like this man, you have a choice. You can choose to replicate that attitude or you can choose how you wish to die. This man decided that he wasn't going to live a living death for ten or twenty years. Instead he was determined to find new interests to pursue and to commit himself to renewing his marriage.

Once you've freed yourself from the temptation to dodge death, you are ready to look at your own life from a transcendent perspective which will help you complete this task of accepting your one and only life.

The Transcendent Perspective

We talked about the transcendent perspective as we considered the death of a spouse in Chapter 6. That perspective is just as important as you make peace with your own mortality. As before, we will express that perspective by giving you two dichotomous statements, one the immature outlook, the other the transcendent perspective.

_____ Death is an end.   _____ Death is a beginning.
When Annie Warden watched her mother slide downhill, Annie believed the first statement. She saw Mom leaving; she saw an end to a woman she loved very much.
In contrast, Carl Warden watched his Bess walk away down

a road he himself would take. He would grieve, of course.
The sadness would rip his heart and soul. But he could celebrate, too, that death was a gate for his beloved Bess into
eternal life.

Many who study death and dying claim that a death should
be celebrated just as much as a birth. Both are the starts of a
new life. This is reflected in trends recently of people request-
ing an upbeat atmosphere at their funerals. Texas statesman
John Tower requested that the Hallelujah Chorus from Han-
del's *Messiah* be sung at his funeral. He wanted something
joyous and triumphant.

In times past, when most people died at home, the persons
in attendance could sense the dying's attitude about life and
death just in the way they physically let go.

In contrast, attendants have reported that some dying persons grab the sheets, grab people—literally, physically strug-
gling to avoid that final, fearful moment. Decades before
their physical deaths, persons may grab onto spouses, adult
children, friends, or material things, and fear intensely letting
go. Wynn, the man who spent his last years in the nursing
home where he had served as handyman, was unconsciously
wrapping himself up completely and codependently in his
wife: "If I hang onto people around me tightly enough, I'll
never have to say good-bye." Anything that pried Wynn loose
from that grip, such as his residential removal to a nursing
home, placed him in the mortal danger he so desperately tried
to avoid.

We invite you to think about this time of grief and celebration, not in a morbid way but in anticipation. Discuss
with your spouse what you would like your own funeral to
be and listen to your spouse's feelings on the subject. Here,
believe it or not, is still another opportunity for improved
intimacy and oneness. Rites of passage are properly planned
by the persons undergoing those rites, be they funerals or
weddings.

_____ Death invalidates life.   _____ Death completes life.

Let us tell you the story of two patients. The first woman had devoted her whole life to nurturing her children, her grandchildren, occasional nieces and nephews and a foster child as well. Through time she became less and less necessary to the younger generation. There came a day when they didn't need her at all. They didn't want her to baby-sit; too old, they implied. They didn't need her cookies. Her quaint clothes and clicking false teeth embarrassed the teenaged grandkids. What was the use of living, when it was all gone to naught like this?

The second grandmother, equally as dedicated to the children and grandchildren, took the transcendent view. She celebrated that the children didn't need her anymore. That indicated she had raised them well, sending them out into the world fully equipped to take what comes. She had done a good job; she had completed her role. She could relax now after a job well done, and enjoy the peace of not having to take care of youngsters.

Both women's circumstances were identical. Each saw their role in life as a caregiver, a nurturer. When that role was no longer applicable, one felt her life was no longer valid. The other, instead, was able to surrender that role without being threatened. The difference in their responses? Perspective.

The second woman saw this passage of her life as a time of transition, not between passages, but between this life and the next. She seemed to see God as she never had before.

Obviously, none of us can see God directly. God Himself told Moses that the Israelites would die if they saw His face. That's a condition we have to accept as part of our mortality. For this life, we see Him indirectly through images.

We've found that many people in Passage Five see six images of God as they never have before. What was pure theology in their twenties and thirties becomes the essence of their existence in their seventies and eighties. This is the transition period where I've not left earth yet, but I am beginning to experience God and the Holy Spirit within me in a deeper way. That's why many cultures revere older people. They instinctively know they are more spiritual than younger people, a bonus of Passage Five.

Image One: God as Father

To patients who've missed their dad's parental nurturing, to those who've had an especially difficult marriage or childhood, to those who've had to say a premature good-bye to their spouses, this image of God is particularly reassuring. It's as if they are coming full circle. They emerged out of the womb and into a family headed by earthly parents. Now they are going back into the womb to join their heavenly family. Good-bye to the stern, remote earthly father. Hello to the loving heavenly Father.

The second grandmother saw herself returning to that family, rather than ending her life. Her heavenly family was becoming as important—if not more important—than her earthly family. She knew the crossover would be scary, just as the births of her children were scary and painful, yet joyous. God was increasingly near.

Image Two: As a Shepherd, Someone Who Leads

Often it's difficult for older men and women to surrender their positions of leadership and responsibility. The man or woman who was the head of a corporation or a department or a region of the country is now without that challenge. Those grandmothers are no longer responsible for their children or grandchildren. They are no longer shepherds.

Once older people come to see God as their shepherd, they no longer maintain a death grip on the rod and staff. They're not humiliated to lay down those symbols of power. Instead, they see this as a natural transition and feel a tremendous sense of relief since they no longer feel false guilt about not being super-productive. It's not difficult for them to allow

God to shepherd them through Passage Five and back home again.

Image Three: God as a Physician and Healer

Those in Passage Five obviously feel their physical morality. Some are just slowing down. Others live with constant pain or are confined to a wheelchair.

Chronic or terminal illness doesn't seem like a dirty trick to people who know they can trust God to ease their pain and feel it may soon be time to lay down their physical bodies. They know that as part of their salvation they shall have new, purified bodies in eternity.

Robert Hemfelt remembers his mother, who in her mid-seventies suffered hip pain, teasing about her aches and pains. "I'm getting ready to lay down this body," she would say. "After all, it's got a lot of mileage on it. It's time to trade it in."

After she suffered a heart attack and experienced kidney failure, the doctors told her they could keep her alive indefinitely on dialysis. She and her husband prayed about the alternative. She opted to forego heroic measures and let nature have its way. Said she, "My body is a vehicle I picked up at birth, and I'll lay it down at death." Together, the elder Hemfelts began a two-week death watch, a peaceful waiting for her homegoing.

Image Four: God as Judge

It might seem strange for this image of God to be comforting to someone who knows eternity is all too close. Yet we find that patients are often relieved of bitterness during the Fifth Passage. One acquaintance, for instance, spent years feeling angry because her cousin inherited mineral-rich land from a family member and she received pasture land from that same relative. For years she was obsessed by the injustice of it all. "Now in my sixties, it doesn't bother me so much," she tells us. "I can't explain why. Nothing has changed, legally or physically. She still has the mineral rights; I still have rocks and grass. Yet it doesn't matter as much. God might just have a perspective on this that I can't see just now." People who have been wronged by other people clearly picture that Judge whose justice is beyond human justice. All these inequities are known to Him, they know, and are being worked out on a cosmic level we someday will understand.

Sometimes in our group sessions we tease patients. "Sitting here in group, we're experiencing a little taste of heaven. Together we can look back on our lives—including the pain of our childhood—and realize, 'We're all doing the best we know how.' Instead of bitterness, we can forgive each other and feel a sense of justice and resolution and forgiveness about what happened. Someday we will all face each other in Heaven and be able to forgive in this same way."

Image Five: God as Savior and Redeemer

Where does it all end up? The non-believer possesses no good hope at all. The believer? All the believer's life, she has been talking about faith. Have faith. Help faith grow. It's almost all talk, but not because of hypocrisy. Only in these last years does spiritual surrender become truly possible. All friends, all relatives, perhaps even the spouse—all, all fall away. No more props, far fewer distractions.

"Uplifting disillusionment," Dr. Hemfelt calls it. "It's the final grief and acceptance that no earthly savior or parent or spouse will ever completely fulfill your needs in life. At last, you can turn your hands and heart completely to God."

People in Passage Five also become very aware of what they have done to others. For years they may have rationalized—or denied—their physical abuse of one of their children, but now, as they watch their grandchildren go through the same rebellion, they are flooded with waves of guilt and remorse and shame. They are ready to say, as the prophet Isaiah did, "Thank You, Lord, that You have said: 'I, even I, am He who blots out your transgressions for My own sake; and I will not remember your sins' (Isa. 43:25).''

Spiritual resolution of the deepest sort, the sort that leads to a true and abiding love of God, comes only when the person has said all the other good-byes, made peace with his or her life, and has put away all the false idols that used to call so temptingly.

All the substitutes are at last put away; will the real God please stand up?

If this passage goes well, a strong spiritual base permits peace. Carl Warden could say good-bye to Bess. He could face his own pending death honestly and squarely. The last goodbye. A new and transcendent love and peace with God: the ultimate hello.

How Well Have You Accepted Your One and Only God-Given Life?

Take a moment to consider your own situation. How well have you achieved a transcendent perspective and accepted your life as it is today? How are you feeling about your death? What about that of your spouse? Check the statements below that apply to you to measure your progress. Have your spouse do the same. Then come together to discuss them.

_____ "I can still give the world something." It is:

_____

_____

_____

_____ "I can picture myself as an old person and (barring unpredictable catastrophic illness) can pretty much estimate what my physical and mental limitations might be. I may not

be completely at peace with the vision, but I can see it."
Those limitations might be:

_____

_____

_____

   "God's role in my life, particularly as it applies to death and
illness, is:

_____ ."

(For instance, some of our patients feel that God has been
guiding each day of their life. They are often able to face
death well, because they know He has held them before
through difficult situations and they know He will hold them
again. They trust Him as they trust no one else.)

_____

_____

_____

   "My attitude toward death is:
   _____ I am petrified of death. It seems like the final end."
   _____ I'd rather die now than live another year of misery."
   _____ I am prepared for my own death when that time may
come."
   _____ I look forward to saying 'Hello' to my God."
   _____ I believe Jesus Christ saved me from my sins and that
I will live with Him forever."

   If you are afraid of death, you need to ask yourself why. We
always find that someone who is haunted by a strong appre-
hension about death has an underlying fear about life and
living. One woman referred her mother to us. The grandmother had become possessive and paranoid about money.
She was afraid someone was going to swindle her. She was
afraid her money wouldn't last the rest of her lifetime. She
was afraid someone was trying to get control of her money.
   In reality the woman had more than enough money to last
a lifetime, and she couldn't put her wealth in a U-Haul® and

attach it to a hearse. In counseling she realized that her fear of death, and her paranoia about money, reflected her childhood fears of not having enough to eat during the Great Depression. She grieved that former fear and accepted her mortality.

You are now well familiar with the grieving process. Hardly morbid, grieving your mortality frees you to accept God's ultimate plan for you. No longer fretting and dreading the inevitable, you are able to live the years ahead with a new freedom. And, you can provide that unique, very necessary perspective to the younger generation.

Chapter 9

Your Opportunity to be a Mentor

*I*t was a few months before Bess Warden's illness was diagnosed that Carl Warden and Alan, his grandson-in-law, sat chatting on the back porch of Carl and Bess's home.

Carl hefted his coffee mug. "More?" he asked Alan.

"Uh, no thanks. I have a question. It's, uh, rather personal."

"Shoot."

"We learned in college that when a marriage partner dies, the survivor tends to romanticize the relationship. He or she paints the picture of the past much rosier that it actually was. I know that Beth Anne and I think everything is terribly romantic now. It's a lot of fun. Now I'm scared it's going to wear off. It didn't seem to wear off for you two, though. Beth Anne and Annie both say you and Bess have been perpetual newlyweds your whole marriage. How did you manage?"

Perpetual newlyweds? Hardly. Carl shook his head. "I know for sure, if you leave a marriage to its own devices, you'll drift apart."

"Experts agree on that. So how do you avoid the drifting?"

Carl pondered that question for a few minutes. He sipped his coffee; it was stone-cold. "You start out naive. You commit yourself to marriage not knowing what the blazes you're getting into. No matter what you think it's gonna be—no

160

matter what your dreams are—it turns out to be something different. I guess. . . I guess, you commit yourself to go with the flow, whatever the flow ends up being."

"Commitment to stick with it?"

Carl nodded. "And commitment to stick with it *together*; I mean really together. Not just to stay undivorced but to stay truly married." A thought struck him suddenly. "You don't marry a dream or a way of life; you marry a person. The dream might change, the way of life probably will, and the person certainly will. And so will you. We all do. Your commitment is to that person all the while you're both changing."

Alan frowned. "You mean you consciously adapt to each other?"

"I doubt you do it consciously, at least not much. Bess and I got off the track a couple of times. Found ourselves drifting away. The conscious part is seeing what's happening and taking steps to bring yourselves back together.

"You're gonna grow, regardless. So when you see yourself growing apart, sit down and figure out how to grow together."

Alan received much more advice like that from Carl over the next few months following his wedding—valuable advice only available from a man who had been there, had experienced it firsthand, and knew the ropes. Carl Warden was just such a man.

You, too, as you enter and experience the Fifth Passage can provide just as sage advice to the younger generations. You've been through the hoops, you know where the pitfalls are, you may even have experienced them yourself, and you're starting to see the transcendent perspective to life. What better position to be in as a mentor?

Brian Newman points out, "A lot of men and women in their twenties and thirties seek out the wisdom of elders because they need it so. How do I get along? What do I do now? What does all this mean? Only older, wiser persons can fill that need. Mentoring is an important and valuable gift older people in any passage can give persons younger than themselves."

What is involved specifically? Says Brian, "A mentor has information and emotions in his or her background that were lacking in many people's childhoods, things that ought to be there but weren't. Younger people are looking for guidance from a mature mentor to encourage, support, and direct them."

For years, business has been using mentors to prepare the next generation. The principle extends far beyond business.

"A mentor can help shape your character," Brian explains. "He or she is a coach pushing you to improve. The mentor cares enough about you to kick you in the pants and then put his or her arms around you. So many people either missed it growing up or still need it.

"At each passage, we all desire advice and attention from someone in the next stage of marriage. It's a universal need for someone bigger and older, more mature and stronger, who cares and is involved in our life."

Brian believes the generation coming up, the persons less than thirty years old, suffer a dearth of wisdom and information from the preceding generations, more than did people in the past.

A friend in government service sees a loss of connection between the generations. "As older employees are retiring, and upper-level management jobs open up, the ones choosing the personnel who will fill those vacancies seem to be skipping a link. Rather than fill the positions with fifty-year-olds, they are choosing from the thirty- and forty-year-olds. This is fine for the younger persons being promoted, but it breaks the continuity of knowledge.

"Departments find themselves reinventing the wheel over and over, because the older people who already knew about the wheel have left. In my department we keep trying things that don't work. Then we happen to talk to some retired fellow, and he'll say, 'Oh we tried that twenty years ago. It didn't work then, either,' and tell us why. We could have saved a lot of time and money, had he been there to guide us."

How about You?

Do you see any opportunities for mentoring? It need not be in your family. Even if you see none, try to seek out a mentoring situation. Debi Newman warns, "At this stage of life, couples *absolutely* have to avoid seeing themselves as having nothing to share or give. Mentoring is exactly what they can give now and it is one of the most crucial needs in our world today."

As it is with forgiveness, a mentor is benefited just as much or more so than the person you are mentoring. Some of the benefits you might experience by being a mentor are:

Increased Self-Worth

As you found an outlet for all the experience and knowledge you have stored up inside you, your self-esteem builds. None of this phony "let's jack up the old self-esteem, worthy or not" stuff. You are truly doing something worthy for the world. You are being the "wise grandmother" or "wise grandfather" so lauded by eastern cultures. There can be no better contribution to society and the world than your expertise and learning passed on to the next generation.

Active Mind

Mentoring is an excellent way to keep your own mind alert and active. Universally, experienced mentors claim they learn more than they teach. It's simple: you have to stay on top of it all when you counsel and sponsor the next generation. Too, you will find yourself forced to think now, maybe more so than any other time in your life, as you are presented with the perplexing problems of the younger generations.

Too, the transcendent perspective we've so emphasized in

this book will be put into action with this mentoring. You will have a more worldly perspective from which to speak from having lived and gone through all you have over your long and rich life.

Reliving

In a way, by remembering all the lessons you learned—some easy and some not so easy—you will be reliving parts of your life. Just as sharing memories brings intimacy between you and your spouse, so will mentoring. As you recall the hard times when you had your first child or your second or third, those memories will rush back, revitalizing your relationship, rebonding you to each other. The past will prove why you've stayed together this long and how very special this relationship is. This is just as true for memories of a spouse that has already died. It will provide you more fuel for a transcendent perspective as you truly appreciate your life together with your spouse.

Communication from God

It's no secret that God uses those around us to communicate. It's one of the very special privileges of being human—to be a pipeline for God's messages. "We are ambassadors for Christ," boasted Paul. Paul considered us not ambassadors to the young but ambassadors to everybody, even to each other. The young are the Exuberance of God. But we who are old are His Wisdom.

Carl Jung claimed that a person cannot begin to grasp God before the age of thirty-five, halfway through life. He felt that until that time we were too busy and not well enough prepared by life itself. If that is so, or somewhat so, we who are older have a perspective to give younger people that they themselves cannot reach without help. We mentor on a spiritual level above theirs, drawing them upward. What better service can a man or woman in Christ render?

What Can You Give?

How do you know if you have any advice or experience worth sharing? A little introspection will reassure you. Actually, just making it this far qualifies you.

More specifically, think about these things as you wonder what the next generation can draw from you:

1. The prior lifestyle.

"My little Rachel is growing up with a telephone in the car. For her, that's nothing out of the ordinary," Brian Newman speaks with something of a sense of awe.

"In parts of Arkansas where I grew up," Frank Minirth relates, "not even the houses had telephones."

Do you remember when the milkman came around? When you saw your first jet plane? Did you ever fly commercially in a prop plane? What do you recall of the past that is gone now? Those recollections are valuable. Jot down some notes here on things you could talk about with younger kids, particularly kids interested in history:

_____

_____

_____

_____

_____

_____

2. Obsolete ways of doing things.

About the time you think nobody but nobody wants to hear about the old generators in cars, your nephew starts trying to restore a 1949 Packard. Suddenly, you're in demand. Did you ever use an ironer when you were young? Play a treadle organ? Repair the old tube style radios? List some skills no longer required in everyday life that historical societies, restoration groups, museums, and living history programs might be interested in:

_____

_____

_____

_____

_____

_____

3. Dealing with people.

For years, Shawna interviewed prospective employees for a bank security firm. She had to weed out the possible crooks quickly, and she did so by interviewing literally hundreds of people a month. She developed some amazing techniques for drawing information smoothly and efficiently from macho types, gray-haired-mother types, chauvinists—the whole spectrum of humankind. She has a wealth of suggestions and shortcuts for anyone connected with interviewing. You've been around awhile. What are you good at when it comes to handling people?

_____

_____

_____

_____

_____

_____

4. Your special interest.

Everyone has a shtick, an interest or specialty that is unique. A collection (We have a friend who collects penguins. Statues, pictures, porcelain figures, Pittsburgh hockey memorabilia . . .), a skill (Another acquaintance ties knots. Hundreds of amazing knots; he's in great demand at Boy Scout jamborees), an area of expertise. What is yours?

_____

_____

_____

Is someone you know (and this doesn't have to be someone young) hoping to enter a line of work you are either skilled at or once did well? Can you take that person under your wing and help him or her get through the first difficult doors?

And then there's the one job you've been working at for decades—your marriage. Just as there are those that mentor from their job-related experience, there are also those that mentor from their marital experience. Think how much you can help others in prior marriage passages. What can you pass on to the younger generation?

1. What do you believe is the greatest key to staying together in marriage? What worked for you?

_____

_____

_____

2. What do you think is the most harmful thing one can do to destroy a marriage?

_____

_____

_____

3. What are your specific wishes for each of your children and grandchildren?

_____

_____

_____

4. What goals do you have for yourself in the next ten years?

_____

_____

_____

How would your goals help younger marrieds as they set goals?

_____

_____

_____

5. If you had it to do over, what goals would you and your spouse set early on in your marriage?

_____

_____

_____

6. What are some important crises in your marriage that you think your children and grandchildren should know about?

_____

_____

_____

7. What legacy do you want to leave your children regarding your marriage?

_____

_____

_____

Even if you can answer only one of these questions clearly, you have something important to pass on in this day of rapid and unrepentant divorce.

As you thought about the topics above, did the names of anyone in particular come to mind—persons who could perhaps answer the question even better than you, or persons who could benefit from learning what you can offer on a topic? If names came up as persons you want to pass information on to, target them as possible pupils.

A *caveat* is in order here. Do be cautious about forcing your advice and knowledge on unwanting ears. Unwanted advice is just as dangerous as no advice at all, and perhaps more so. If you want a child to peek into a box, you say, "Whatever you do, don't peek in that box!"

You might remember just how much your teenager rebelled against your wishes so many years ago. Human nature prompts us to go in the opposite direction of what we're told to do. So, if you force unwanted advice, you might indirectly lead a person in the opposite direction you meant to.

A mentor relationship is two-way. The pupil seeks, the mentor gives. Keep it that way.

Codifying the Wisdom

Some museums, historical societies, and the like send volunteers out to tape record the stories of older people. It works like this: the museum or group learns of an old-timer with a story or an area of expertise in which that group is very interested. Perhaps an old woman's grandparents came over the Oregon trail, and their stories have been handed down to her. The Nebraska State Historical Society (for instance) sends an interviewer to her home. The interviewer sits her down with a small, unobtrusive tape recorder, and gets her talking about her historically important stories.

Or, a linguistic society sends out trained interviewers to record the dialect and slang of a particular ethnic group or subculture of Americans. . . . of other countries, for that matter. There are writers who specialize in recording folk tales and ethnic stories.

These people are painstakingly building a body of material that seizes elements of the past that are fading away. Quite possibly you can be a part of it on either side of the tape recorder; providing information or gathering information. This is a form of mentoring in which you give your special talents and skills not to one or two persons but to a culture.

Contracting Your Marriage

There is one other area of your interest that ought to be codified.

When we counsel married couples in their first passages, we urge them to build a marital contract.

That's all right for young people. But you have weathered so many storms you surely don't need such a thing as a contract, do you? Actually, you will find a marriage contract a very useful thing.

It can serve as a guide, a goal clarifier, a spur to do what you wish you would do if you got to it . . . all sorts of things. And it's all there in black and white.

Let's look at how you would go about creating one.

Chapter 10

The New Contract/ How Well Have You Done?

"Oh, come on!" you fume. "I'm decades and decades old. Not a new marriage contract at this stage of the game!"

Sure. Why not? Whether your future will be two days or two decades, make it the best future possible.

Throughout our marriage counseling, we encourage couples to build a contract which states specifically what they need, want, and expect from their relationship. Some will honor it religiously and others will hold to it lightly. In either case, the contract clarifies the needs and positions of both spouses.

If you have never created such a contract, it may sound confusing or superfluous. It is neither.

Persons building a marital contract first sketch the broad parameters of what they expect from the union. The very basics. For example, a statement of commitment is basic. "I am committed to perpetuating this union." In all honesty, a person might be compelled to say, "I am committed to maintaining this union at least for another year." Whatever the truth, it should be framed here.

When writing a new contract, couples address the particulars of their individual and communal spiritual life. These particulars are reflected in this workbook page:

My view of God: _____
_____

My spouse's view of God: _____

Our common appreciation of God: _____
_____

Areas in which we can compromise or yield regarding God:
_____
_____

My attitude toward Scripture: _____
My spouse's: _____
Areas of common ground: _____
My attitude toward Jesus Christ: _____
_____

My spouse's: _____
_____

Our common ground: _____
My other views of faith and religion: _____
_____
_____
_____

My spouse's: _____
_____
_____
_____

Our mutual statement of faith and commitment: _____
_____
_____
_____
_____
_____

Sexual matters are not quite so large a part of life now, but
they are important. Wise couples write a pledge of fidelity
into their contract. Will that thwart an affair, however benign
the flirtation may be, if one partner or the other decides to

stray? Of course not. But it reduces the chance of a flirtation beginning by putting in visible, solid, immutable writing, the couple's promise to each other. It reminds, it encourages, it supports.

We suggest that each spouse write a contract independently, working out his and her new agenda and needs. The first drafts may be similar for both persons or quite different. What one partner sees as a big-ticket item may not be significant to the other. One might want better financial boundaries while the other places better cooperation in housekeeping as the top priority. Write down whatever you think you want your partner to understand and agree upon.

Start with broad brush strokes. A statement of faith, so to speak, is a good way to begin. Fidelity? What do you pledge regarding fidelity? What do you pledge regarding service and devotion. (Let's not get flowery here and write what we think the other wants to hear. You must be honest.) Write a statement of your commitment.

From that broad base, then, fine-tune the little things of life. Most couples run the fine-tuning clear down to a statement of how often each month they ought to go out to eat.

Once these individual contracts are drafted, we ask the couples to enter the negotiation phase which like any other arbitration involves some give and take.

Give and take in open negotiation is an excellent way to work around strongly differing agendas. It operates just like union bargaining. "I'll concede this if you'll concede that. I'll give you this point if you'll give me that point."

The final draft of the marriage contract, then, will reflect the fruits of this bargaining. It will contain the statements about the marriage each person has made. Inherent in it is the promise that each partner will abide by that agreement, usually for a specified time. The contract can be renegotiated every year or so if you wish.

We invited May and Gary, the grandparents of Cody, to write for themselves a marriage contract. This contract had

nothing to do with Cody, in theory. It had everything to do
with the marriage itself. We invite you to follow along.

They began with the broad brush strokes:

Your statement of fidelity: _____

_____

Your requests and desires regarding sexual needs: _____

_____

_____

What you feel are your spouse's needs and requests: _____

_____

_____

_____

_____

Then the tough stuff started.

Grandparenting did not mean at all the same thing to May
as it did to Gary. Gary was certain that if they didn't tightly
discipline Cody there would be grief to pay—more grief, in
fact, than what was being paid already. May tended to feel
that a little coddling wouldn't hurt. Let Cody feel loved.
They were on different agendas and absolutely had to make
some adjustments. So Cody ended up a central figure in the
contract after all.

As a matter of fact, as May and Gary worked on their
contract, presumably an agreement affecting only the two of
them, they realized how deeply and intrusively Cody and his
mother were embedded in May and Gary's lives. It was Cody
this and Cody that, at every turn. They were shocked to see
not only how much they were enmeshed with the boy, but
how much of Cody's upbringing their daughter had relegated
to them. The relationship was no longer healthy for either

Cody or May and Gary. They built into the contract an agreement to reverse the polarizing tendency to parent Cody.

Gary never knew that May wanted to get out of the kitchen more often than was happening. He readily agreed, during give-and-take, to take her out to breakfast at least once a week. In return she agreed to be more tolerant of the sawdust messes he made in the kitchen when he built another of his woodworking projects.

Points I want to negotiate for:

_____

_____

_____

_____

_____

_____

Points I am ready to offer in return:

_____

_____

_____

_____

_____

_____

Points my spouse says he or she wants to receive:

_____

_____

_____

_____

_____

_____

Points my spouse is offering in return:

_____

_____

_____

_____

By the time they hammered out the final version, May and Gary knew a lot more about each other than they had guessed before. And that, as you can see, is the ultimate goal of a contract—improved and deepened intimacy.

We have displayed an example of a new marriage contract on page 177. Using it as a general guide, modify it for your own unique situations.

The Goals of Contracts

The bottom line of your marriage contract is the bottom line of any union contract—two entities helping each other succeed and move forward. The antithesis of dysfunction, in marriage as in anything else, is mutual aid, as each helps the other satisfy needs and complete the necessary tasks of each passage.

It is not a goal of the new contract that all parties agree on the same agenda. You may well reach the decision that you have different agendas and different priorities. Matching or meshing diverse agendas in which all parties prosper is just as fine as identical agendas, and perhaps even better.

Be aware that not all meshing agendas are wholesome. These two agendas, for instance, fit:

He: I believe all women should be submissive.

She: I believe all men should be dictatorial.

But no one's going to grow in that relationship. The love, then the respect, and eventually perhaps even the marriage itself, will die.

An example in our counsel recently illustrates unwholesome meshing of agendas. A husband wanted to carve out a vocational identity for himself and the wife declared a contract in which security was the top priority. Those two agendas could mesh nicely, as he built the security of a strong

THE RENEWED MARRIAGE CONTRACT

1. Statement of affirmation; at least one attribute each person admires and appreciates in the other
2. Statement of extent of commitment to the marriage
3. Promise of fidelity
4. Statement of faith, embracing:
   a. Each person's individual statement of faith
   b. Clearly stated common ground
   c. Statement of tolerance (and limits of tolerance)
5. Statement of recognition of old, dysfunctional hidden agendas
6. Declaration of new agendas to redress dysfunctions
7. Sexual contract, including:
   a. Recognition of difficulties or shortcomings in present sexual relations
   b. Steps to improve relations and/or explore new techniques
   c. Details of frequency if frequency is an issue
8. Review of items in first contract, with updates and revisions as necessary
9. Details of everyday life (request for romantic nights out) established through give-and-take (be specific)
10. Agreement on matters associated with children, if appropriate
11. Agreement to review and update contract periodically (anniversaries for instance)

presence on the job. But they became antagonistic, for he spent long hours on overtime and she languished, uncertain of his love. Her concept of security was emotional, his monetary.

One result of clear communication and honest contract negotiation is improved intimacy. You know each other better, understand each other better, appreciate each other better. You can better grasp what makes your marriage tick. You can see harmful influences and work out ways together to combat them. You can see the healthy, positive influences and rejoice in them. Just the act of building a mutually advantageous contract can bind you together more securely.

This concept of contract writing is not a quick fix for anything. You have to do the homework first, all of it. Explore the kind of hidden messages that could be governing your desires and actions without your knowledge. Explore your real feelings toward each other and the marriage. Explore the extent to which you have forgiven, the extent to which you have adequately grieved losses. If you haven't dug out the truths of your emotional and marital life, the surface patch-up will surely fail.

When One Side Refuses

In so many marriages, one partner focuses on change and improvement but the other has no interest or may even sabotage it, desperately afraid of change. Then what?

It is *not* true that a marriage can't change for the better unless both spouses buy into the change.

Because we already know something about Murphy and Myrtle Speis, let's use them in a hypothetical case. Recently retired, Murphy wanted to travel extensively, and Myrtle, still working full-time, was loathe to give up her very satisfying work. So let's pretend that Myrtle was willing to work out a marriage contract but Murphy adamantly refused. He saw it as yielding control, and he would not give up what little control he had. (This is not so hypothetical after all; frequently, spouses in our counsel flatly refuse to cooperate.)

In that case, Myrtle would draw up a new contract stating "How I am choosing to be in this marriage." This automatically cancels the implied contract between the two. So, as Myrtle either sticks to her guns or decides to yield a part of her dream and happiness as a love gift, she can change their relationship—*to an extent*—by changing her half of the contract.

Invitation to the Dance

Let's illustrate that in a different light through a woman we'll call Katherine. Because of the tendency to polarize we've discussed throughout this book, Katherine took on more and more jobs in her marriage that, to an increasing extent, didn't get done if she left them to her husband, Glen. Eventually she was handling the checkbook, the income tax, the mortgage payments, social scheduling, and all medical and legal appointments—not to mention mowing the lawn. Glen didn't deliberately avoid those things; he simply didn't get around to them. Angry and frustrated, she turned to a reliable friend, a friend who didn't seem to have that problem, for advice.

The friend suggested that Katherine consider a stalemate. Katherine mulled that advice carefully. It seemed sound. She acted. "I created a crisis," she later explained. "No, that's not quite it. I let the crisis happen. First I decided what I absolutely wanted to get done. That was appointments involving the kids, income tax, and the mortgage payment. I made certain those things were kept current.

"I told Glen I was handing the rest back to him. Instead of watching sports on TV all night, he could balance the checkbook and some of those things. 'I will no longer do them,' I said. He shrugged it off; I don't think he thought I was serious.

"Chaos. I mean, there was chaos. The checkbook was a mess. He got billed for a dental appointment he made and forgot. He showed up 24 hours late to his boss's hot tub party. The lawn grew so high we kept losing the dog. I stood firm. 'You take some of the responsibility in this outfit,' I told him. 'It's supposed to be a two-person operation.'

"Eventually, it was. I think the turning point was when the bank called him at work and threatened to repossess his pickup truck if he didn't pay up by the close of that day. He delivered the check in person."

Katherine smiles now. "But I was tearing my hair out by

then. It was a learning experience for me too. Now I know that even when only one person forges a new contract, and enforces it, it saps the strength of the old one."

Katherine invited her partner back into the dance. In essence she was doing what AlAnon and other codependency groups have long advocated: Quit enabling. When one person decides not to enable, the other must change. Even if the other party doesn't buy into the new arrangement, crisis develops, and that crisis will force the other party to address the old, ill-fitting contract.

A rank-and-file union worker would explain it another way. "You're talking about a contract walkout. Union and management are forced to negotiate. The union or company may walk out of contract negotiation if they don't see progress. That's not walking out of the company. The person is not walking out of the marriage, right? Just the situation. When you're on strike, something's got to give!"

Strike the Band

Unfortunately, we find strikes happening in marriages all the time, often at the subconscious level, down on the level of those hidden agendas. They are not engaged for constructive purposes, such as the strike Katherine used to advantage, and if they go unrecognized, they may last the balance of the marriage. Over the years, you may have had one or more operating in your own marriage.

A very common one we find is the woman who goes on strike sexually. "I'm cooking for you and doing your laundry. But no eroticism." A common way for the husband to go on strike is to stop participating in family affairs. "I'm the breadwinner, and I'm still here," but not at the little league game, the family picnic, or whatever. Usually if one or the other party is on strike, it has something to do with unresolved, unfinished anger. If the strike is not recognized and alleviated, any new contract will be just a paper-exercise in futility. Anger resolved and redirected in a positive way is healthy.

Katherine's strike was born of anger, but her strike was not an end in itself, and certainly not intended to punish Glen for wrongs real or imaginary. Her goal was healthy change. A strike without such a goal is futile and destructive.

On page 182 is an example of what a new marriage contract might look like specifically tailored for a Fifth Passage marriage. Use it as a very general guideline and then prepare one unique to your relationship. We suggest that your renewed marriage contract address the following areas as broad, general parameters.

Adjust for a Life Without Each Other

Financially

Knowing the end was near, Mary Alice's father set up a good financial plan for his wife. He had handled the finances throughout their life together and he did it now. In your case, you may wish for one person to do it or both to do it together. But write it in. In practical ways: Can your spouse negotiate the stairs in the house? How about tomorrow? Can your spouse reach the top shelves in the pantry? Can he or she safely use the bathroom facilities? Take care of yard work? Can your spouse do all the ordinary everyday activities without your physical help? Is now the time to look at a smaller, ground-floor-only dwelling? Contract for your future dwelling according to the needs of you both. Now's the time to get tough with each other about such practical matters.

Brian's grandparents live in a neighborhood that has changed around them. It began as a neighborhood of people their own age, background, and financial status. All that is different now. Because they owned their home and loved it, they stayed, until the fabric of the neighborhood altered so much they became outsiders. They don't feel free to visit friends. They're not as mobile as they might be elsewhere. Consider your own circumstance. If it's similar to theirs,

The New Marriage Contract
Fifth Passage

1. Statement of Affirmation; at least one attribute each person admires and respects in the other
2. Statement of Commitment; a sentence or paragraph describing how each person promises to foster and renew intimacy with the other
3. Statement of Faith, embracing:
   a. Each person's individual statement of faith
   b. Clearly stated common ground
   c. Statement of tolerance (and limits of tolerance) for differences in faith between the two of you
4. Statement of plans for a life without the other
   a. Financial plans - wills, residences, funerals, life and health insurance, annuities
   b. Emotional plans - needs, wants, desires, support
5. Statement of commitment to help the world around you
   a. Charitable causes
   b. Mentoring
6. Statement of mutual growth
   a. Practical - outings, books, foods, friends
   b. Emotional - physical relationship, intimacy building
   c. Spiritual - commitment to foster transcendence in each other
7. Statement of any dysfunctional hidden agendas needing resolution and ways to resolve those agendas before it's too late
8. Review of items in any prior marriage contract, with updates and revisions as necessary
9. Details of everyday life (request for alone time and couple time) established through give and take
10. Commitment to periodically review and update contract (annually is best and anniversaries are a good time)
11. Statement of recognition of each other's mortality, and place for responding to the death of the other spouse

should you bite the bullet and change your residence, your neighborhood, your style of living? Write it in.

Make it a contract item to keep the will up to date, as well as any preliminary funeral arrangements, if you so choose. Most funeral homes will help you make arrangements in advance of need. Though it sounds grisly, it relieves the surviving spouse of much additional stress, confusion, and heartache. If you've not formulated a will yet, by all means do so now. Contract to put everything in writing. Everything. Quite probably your executor will not be able to honor oral requests. Put them on paper.

Emotionally

How do you want your spouse to help you prepare emotionally for what is coming? Write it in as a specific contract point. Listen carefully to what your spouse expresses as needs. Explain your own needs clearly. Then discuss how best you can help each other.

Decide What to Give the World

There are a lot of people and causes who can still use you, and use you in two capacities. You can pray, and you can participate—Lord willing, you can do both.

Wise Christians write their prayer life right into the contract. How exactly will each spouse be accountable to the other regarding prayer? How does the wife want her man to pray for her; how does he want her to pray for him? What causes and persons are one spouse's concern only, and which are mutual concerns? United prayer works miracles.

Write in your contract just what each of you plans to do (usually on a weekly basis) for a cause or charity. That cause or charity might be something far-reaching and international in scope. It might be your own son or granddaughter right here who's having problems and needs a temporary hand.

The vital role of mentoring we discussed in the last chapter should be written right into your contract. Include any areas where you are mentoring and commit to continue with this service. If neither of you is a mentor, then write into the contract that you will actively seek out opportunities to become one—perhaps through your church, your local school, or even your family. Mentoring can benefit relatives or friends or, best of all, they can benefit both.

Contract for Growth

Write in some sort of accountability toward each other regarding horizons. Help each other prevent your horizons from diminishing. Keep each other growing. Sample statements: "We will try at least one new food every month." "We will try a new ethnic restaurant each month." "We will each check out at least two books per week from the library or bookmobile, books neither of us have read before."

Intimacy should still be growing too. You're not too old for touching and hugging, even if sexual potency has abated. Unless you do a lot of spontaneous hugging and caressing, write into the contract a minimal amount of such closeness. Five minutes of hugging a day, at least, or whatever both of you feel comfortable with.

Revision

Make certain you write into the contract a specified time each year to review it. Most financial counselors ask you to review your program annually. Doctors expect you to get an annual physical, a pap smear, an occasional mammogram. These are all preventive steps designed to catch small problems and correct them while they are still small. It's the same way with your contract.

You should update your will if your circumstances change, or when a new grandchild or great grandchild enters the family. Update your contract as well.

How Well Have We Done?

Take a moment to gauge your marriage's progress to date. Brian and Debi Newman use questionnaires to do just this with their clients. The answers indicate where in the parade of marriage passages a relationship might be.

Look over the following questions. They are organized by the various tasks we have discussed so far. We invite you to Xerox™ this portion of the book. Have your spouse answer the questions separate from yourself. Then make a special date to go over both your results together. See if there are any areas that need improvement and then work earnestly on them. There is no time like the present to resolve any difficulties.

Task One: Prepare for Retirement
Check those statements that apply to your marriage now as you see it:

_____ "We have a workable plan for our retirement years."
_____ "I am emotionally ready to retire."
_____ "We have established boundaries for the retirement years together. Both of us are satisfied by the personal space we have or will have."
_____ "I see retirement as a positive experience where our marriage can thrive and grow."
_____ "I have grieved any career goals and dreams that have not been achieved."
_____ "I see retirement as a beginning rather than an end. I look forward to this rewarding productive time in my life."
_____ "We have talked about retirement and agree how we will spend those years. We have prepared an allocation chart for our retirement." (Hint: reread Chapter 2 if you don't remember what an allocation chart is.)
_____ "If one partner has desires for retirement and the

other doesn't share them, that one partner has permission to pursue them on his/her own."

_____ "We are flexible enough to accept whatever the future provides for us in our retirement."

_____ "There are still some very important goals that we want to pursue in our retirement; individual and couple goals."

Look back over your responses as well as your spouse's. Do they agree? If not, focus on those statements where you didn't agree. These are the areas that still need attention as you prepare for or experience your retirement years. Perhaps most important, you both should go through the exercise of preparing an allocation chart like we discussed in Chapters 2 and 3.

Task Two: Continue Renewing Love
Check the following statements if they apply to your marriage. Again, have your spouse do the same. Then regroup to check your answers.

_____ "My spouse is my best friend."

_____ "I have other friends apart from my wife/husband."

_____ "I don't limit my outside interests because of fear that my spouse will be upset."

_____ "We maintain strong personal identities within our marriage. We have not become a parent/child relationship."

_____ "I have put away my old dream that my spouse can fulfill every need I have. Completely put it away."

_____ "I don't feel isolated in my marriage and home."

_____ "I recognize the dangers of isolating ourselves from the outside world."

_____ "We both make equal efforts to have other relationships and maintain those friendships outside of our marriage."

_____ "I can name three friends with whom I'd like to

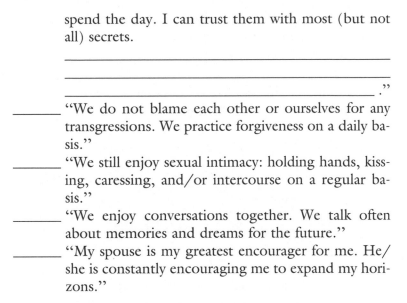

spend the day. I can trust them with most (but not all) secrets.

_____

_____

_____ ."

_____ "We do not blame each other or ourselves for any transgressions. We practice forgiveness on a daily basis."

_____ "We still enjoy sexual intimacy: holding hands, kissing, caressing, and/or intercourse on a regular basis."

_____ "We enjoy conversations together. We talk often about memories and dreams for the future."

_____ "My spouse is my greatest encourager for me. He/she is constantly encouraging me to expand my horizons."

How well did the both of you do on Task Two? Have you managed to foster a renewed intimacy between you? If you could check all, if not most, of these statements you probably have an intimate relationship. Consider yourselves fortunate for intimacy is one of the hardest emotions to maintain in a marriage. If there were statements that you couldn't check, go back over the items we covered in Chapter 5 and talk about them. Talking about each other's feelings, needs, and desires is one of the best ways to foster intimacy. Now is the time to remove the barriers and walls we put up from others. It's time to break those walls down and get to the other side. Do it now before you leave this world. You may never get another chance.

Dr. Minirth explains, "Intimacy is the common goal of any marriage no matter what passage. We are meant to be intimate with one another."

Meant by whom? By God. As Debi Newman puts it, "God didn't see fit to have man alone, even though he was in the Garden of Eden. So he made woman to be with man. Hide from each other behind walls and facades, then, we hide from God. He wanted us to be intimate with one other. It's the only way true sharing and communication can occur."

Task Three: Achieve a Transcendent Perspective
Peruse the following statements to gauge your progress toward this Task Three goal. Check those that reflect your current relationship and state of mind.

_____ "I recognize myself in a perspective that I didn't in my younger days."

_____ "As I look back on my life, I am discovering now what is most important. What I value now is different than what I did before."

_____ "I believe that suffering creates new places in the human heart and soul for love and joy."

_____ "I now realize that the pitfalls I suffered helped build my character and personality."

_____ "I struggle with loneliness at times. But I maximize the opportunities with others by sharing from my heart and soul."

_____ "I appreciate my personal possessions, but I have changed my perception of them. Those that society says are valuable may not be in my eyes. Some of my most valued possessions are those with little monetary worth."

_____ "Even though the years are passing by, time seems eternal now."

_____ "I definitely take the time to 'smell the roses.' "

_____ "My spouse and I have talked about the fact that one of us may leave the other because of death. Neither of us are overcome by excessive fear from this realization."

_____ "I sure don't look forward to it, but I'm prepared to lose my spouse when the time comes."

_____ "I can picture three things I would do for myself, should I lose my spouse in the next ten years:

_____

_____

_____ ."

_____ "We have made financial arrangements for a life without the other."

_____ "We each have individual goals for what we want to leave the world as our legacy."

Possibly the hardest, but the most rewarding experiences of this Fifth Passage is this transcendent perspective. It seems to be the epitome of a human life; what we were born to learn. Help each other in any way possible to achieve this perspective. It's the protection God gives you against the forthcoming losses.

Task Four: Accept My One and Only God-Given Life

What an encompassing task this is! Scores of books, lectures, and sermons have preached this. Look over the following statements to see how you've done with this acceptance and appreciation of your life.

_____ "I feel at peace with God."

_____ "I have grieved the losses in my life and resolved the anger, fear, or denial I have felt."

_____ "I have accepted my one and only God-given life and all the good and bad choices I made in this life."

_____ "I do not think and talk about my physical ailments all the time."

_____ "I still believe that there is hope through God in the world despite the desperate condition of the world and its people."

_____ "There are times that I yearn to be with God in heaven, but I do not think about taking my own life."

_____ "I don't see myself as running away from death."

_____ "I see death as a beginning, not an end."

_____ "God is my guide both now, on earth, and in the future, in heaven."

_____ "I have made amends and resolved any relationships with those people I have wronged."

_____ "I continue to grow and learn more about God each day."

Far easier written about than done is acceptance of your life as it is. Fortunately, as you grow closer to the day you will physically join God, your acceptance of this life increases. If you couldn't check most of these above statements, look carefully at those statements that are blank. Are there any areas you need to work on? How about resolving any relationships? We talked at length about this in our book on the Fourth Passage, *Renewing Love* (Nashville: Thomas Nelson, 1993). Can you think of any relationships that need mending? Have you always wanted to say something to someone and never did? If that person is still available, by all means do so now.

Therapists agree that the more a person does to resolve a relationship with another, the easier that death is on the survivor. That goes equally for your spouse. Say what needs saying, now not later. Now!

Nowhere to Go but Forward

This book concludes our progression of the passages. You have made it home now, scored a crucial run and won the game. One of every two marriages can't say that. You truly deserve a celebration worthy of any World Series victory. Longer than a baseball season, you've managed to overcome the valleys and climb the peaks of a fruitful, rewarding life together. Congratulate yourselves and celebrate.

Does this mean you're done now? Not at all. We'd be surprised if you checked all the statements in our quiz. There are bound to be areas you can still work on. And, don't forget that times, circumstances, and most of all, people change. What works now may not in the future. Use your marriage contract as a commitment to change together, adapt to each other's needs, and continue to grow in this Fifth Passage.

And if one of you leaves for the hereafter, remember, marriage is cyclic and non-age-dependent. Who says a person can't start all over again if he/she gets the chance?

Back Again

Carl Warden hated to see a grown man cry, himself least of all. But the tears ran freely down his cheeks now, as Diane came down the aisle. Praise God, she was beautiful! Warm, suntanned skin, long silver hair swept back in loose, elegant waves; that uncertain, nervous smile. She was almost as beautiful as Bess had looked. He, with a married granddaughter, was himself getting married—how young does that make you feel? He glanced over at his daughter, Annie. The daughter of the groom still had that look of I've-got-it-all-together, and Carl knew that now it was genuine. Annie had come to terms with her marriage and her life, and was making them both work.

Diane stood at his side now, and Carl almost got cold feet. Almost. Diane wasn't taking Bess's place. No one ever could. Bess had been gone over a year now, but she was still as much a part of his life as his memories. She was so many of them. But Diane . . . . Beautiful woman, sprightly companion. For the last year Carl had felt like a centenarian with a hundred-pound backpack, incredibly burdened and incredibly empty. Then he met Diane.

Man is not meant to be alone, the Scripture declares. Carl knew that now. Marriage is so much more than a legal union or a sexual union or a melding of minds and families—infinitely more. "I don't plan to marry again," Diane told him when first they met. "It's just too difficult to break a new one in." And she was serious when she said it. Now here she stood. She felt the pull as much as he did.

Exasperating, elating, horrible, wonderful, shackling, freeing, the human being's single most intimate source of conflict and of joyous intimacy. Marriage.

Carl slipped the ring onto her finger.

"I do."